TABLE OF CONTENTS

TABLE OF FIGURES

CHAPTER ONE

INTRODUCTION

Since the Sheik Said rebellion of 1924, the Turkish republic has waged a nearly continuous counter-insurgency campaign against its Kurdish minority. From 1984 to the present, the campaign has focused exclusively on the Kurdistan Worker's Party (PKK) that has come to represent the nationalist sentiment, if imperfectly, of the ethnic Kurds inside Turkey. In the intervening 81 years, the Turkish government has been unable to eliminate the PKK or Kurdish nationalists as a threat to its security while the Kurds and PKK have been similarly unsuccessful in achieving its objectives of autonomy or independence. The persistent futility of these efforts can be traced to two inter-related causes. The first was the development of the Turkish political culture shaped by the Ottoman Empire coupled with the unique brand of nationalism introduced by Mustafa Kemal Ataturk, the founder of the modern Turk republic. The second factor was the historical relationship between the Kurds and the Ottoman Empire and how this relationship evolved in the new Turkish Republic. The cultural peculiarities of both the Turkish Republic and the Kurdish population have shaped this conflict. The evolution of political structures in this cultural context, or their failure to evolve with changing conditions, had a direct impact on how the state responded to this challenge of ethnic nationalism. This paper addresses how cultural traits can drive the development of solution sets to national problems, particularly in the formulation of policy to address internal problems. It will also suggest ways culture may be exploited to achieve operational objectives.

The development of the Turkish state may be understood as a political entity suspended between three influential forces and encapsulated by one over-riding theme. The Turkish state is suspended between the powerful and competing influences of Islam, Westernization and nationalism while ultimately surrounded by the legacy of the Ottoman Empire. The state's political course has been guided by the need to moderate all three forces and to take its Ottoman history into consideration. Together, these elements form what will be hereafter termed as the Turkish Construct

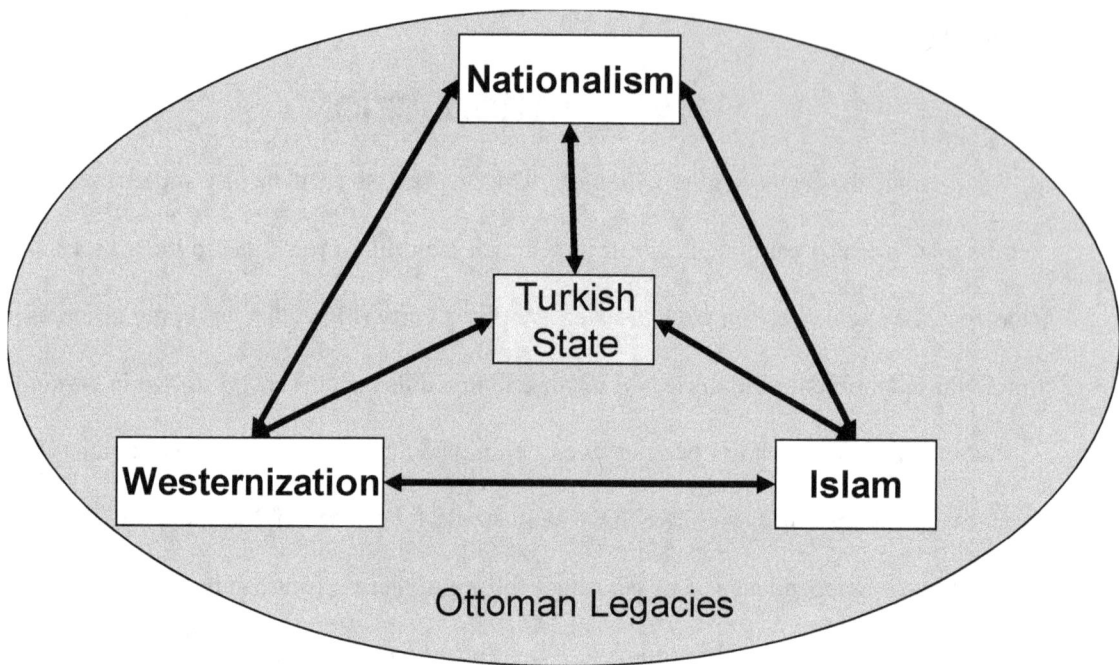

Figure 1. **The Turkish Construct represents the Turkish State suspended between the powerful and competing influences of Westernization, nationalism, and Islam while encompassed in the legacies of the Ottoman Empire.**

[See Figure 1]. Many characteristics of the modern Turkish state have their origins in those of the Ottoman Empire. Therefore, modern manifestations of policy cannot be understood unless its Ottoman context is understood. Similarly, the origins of current policies cannot be understood unless the considerations of nationalism, Islam, and Westernization are overlaid on them. The three influences, bounded by the Ottoman legacies, have directly shaped the Turkish response to Kurdish nationalism within its borders by limiting its perceived options. Kurdish nationalism is considered a direct challenge to the foundations of the republic, and Turkish policymakers have pursued its eradication in an uncompromising manner. This now predictable and often one-dimensional approach, has allowed the Kurds to persist in their struggle as they are unable to achieve their goals yet have been able to still find gaps in the Turkish policies to perpetuate the conflict. This paper offers an analysis of the Turkish Construct in order to reveal how the Turkish state developed its solution set to deal with the PKK and how Kurds have taken advantage of the state's peculiarities in its insurgency.

The cultural uniqueness of each protagonist has also created a fairly novel occurrence in the history of insurgent warfare. Both sides have met degrees of success while violating the accepted fundamentals of both guerrilla and counter-insurgency warfare. The theories of revolutionary Mao Tse-tung and counter-insurgency expert David Galula, while helpful in understanding the generalities of this kind of war, both failed to accurately describe the Turk-Kurd encounter. Galula, an able theorist and practitioner of counter-insurgency posited eight steps to a successful campaign. His eight step process was outlined as follows: (1) concentrate enough forces to destroy or expel insurgent field forces, (2) detach sufficient strength to keep the insurgent from returning, (3) establish contact with the local population, (4) destroy the local insurgent political organization, (5) set up new authorities via elections, (6) test new authorities and replace them if necessary, (7) educate leaders, and (8) win over or suppress the remaining insurgents.[1] The Turkish state had, in a military sense, met the requirements of these precepts, but was unable to completely eradicate the threat. Similarly, the PKK followed Mao's two principles of having a clearly defined goal and gaining the support of the populous, but the Kurds remained far from meeting their objectives. Mao and Galula's models failed as useful guides because they do not encompass the cultural aspects particular to this encounter. Each side in the conflict did not adapt the respective models to fit the cultural constraints and the overall political context in which the war took place.

This paper will address the impact of the Ottoman-Turkish political culture on the conduct of the Turkish counter-insurgency campaign. It will also discuss the Kurdish position vis-à-vis the Turkish culture and state and how this defined their prosecution of a guerrilla war. These cultural characteristics will be compared with the theoretical models of insurgent warfare to determine how they affected the overall conduct of the war. Chapters 2 and 3 will develop the formation of the

---

[1] David Galula, *Counter-Insurgency Warfare: Theory and Practice* (St. Petersburg: Hailer, 2005), 80.

Turkish Construct. Chapter 2 deals with the political evolution of the Ottoman Empire, the role Islam played within it, details its troublesome efforts to modernize, and presents the enduring Ottoman characteristics that are evident in the Turkish Republic. Chapter 3 completes the presentation of the Turkish Construct by analyzing how the disintegration of empire and Kemal Ataturk's brand of nationalism created a new republic. This analysis is performed by viewing the development of the new political structure through the lenses of secularism, modernization and nationalism within the historical Ottoman identity. Chapter 4 discusses how international considerations shaped policy and strategic options on both sides. Chapter 5 is the operational analysis of the Turkish campaign. Using the elements of national power as a model, the chapter addresses the program of action designed and executed by Turkish officials in the diplomatic, informational, military and economic fronts. Chapter 6 briefly addresses revolutionary war theory and details the cultural and political development of the Kurds. Finally, in Chapter 7, the theoretical shortcomings are addressed and potential courses of action are recommended that Turkish and Kurdish leaders could adopt to resolve their differences. Suggested lessons for American operational planners are also presented.

CHAPTER TWO

Ottoman Legacy – History and Political Structure

Much of the history of the Ottoman Empire was characterized by the gradual subjugation of the divergent desires of individual tribes to a central, common authority. The Seljuk tribes were the first Turkic peoples to venture west from the banks of the Aral Sea. These tribes were nomadic and of a warrior class commonly referred to as *ghazi*.[2] It was conquest and the spoils of war that lured these tribal peoples into Mesopotamia where they first encountered Islam and conquered Baghdad, then seat of the Caliphate, in 1055. Converting to Sunni Islam, they gave their elites the title of "Sultan" signifying they were the worldly power of the caliphate.[3] The Seljuks gradually continued their conquests to the west claiming Jerusalem in 1071 and Syria in 1076. Establishing an orderly administration or governmental system was not on the Seljuk agenda and the tribal divisions of these conquerors precluded any such administration from forming as spoils, power and riches continued to be the sole motivators for conquest. After surviving the Mongol invasion and occupation from 1243 to 1335, one tribe rose to assert itself over the Seljuk peoples. This tribe, the Ottomans (so named after its leader, Osman) made significant strides in breaking the tribal divisions and create a centralized rule over the related tribes. This conversion process was largely aided by adaptation of a pre-existing Middle Eastern practice called the *ikta* or slave rule army.[4] Altering the traditional notions of the division of the spoils of war, the Ottomans expanded their ability to subjugate and rule by impressing loyal, armed slaves to maintain order in provinces they themselves were not able to garrison. In addition to controlling conquered lands, this augmentation of physical power allowed them to fend off competing tribes and further consolidate their position. Rule through the threat or use of force became a central component to Ottoman governance.

---

[2] Justin McCarthey, *The Ottoman Turks* (New York: Longman, 1997), 16.
[3] McCarthey, *The Ottoman Turks,* 52.
[4] McCarthey, *The Ottoman Turks,* 16.

Suppression of the fragmented tribal structure took nearly two hundred years and consolidation of the Ottoman system would take an additional two hundred. Historian Justin McCarthey cited this gradual augmentation of institutional capability as a critical Ottoman strength. He offered that "One reason for Ottoman success has to be the slow development of empire…the Ottomans developed their empire over a long period, starting small and growing large. This gave them time to assimilate the peoples they had conquered and to alter their governing methods to meet the needs of an expanded state."[5] In addition to assimilating the conquered lands, the Sultans had the perpetual need to protect their gains from the still powerful tribes of the *ghazi* or nomadic warrior tradition.[6] Murat I, the third Sultan, understood the need for a source of power independent from the tribal system. He would establish the system that would become the hallmark of Ottoman administration and forever link Turkish civil administration with military power.

Murat I expanded on the *ikta* system by making it a source of personal power and a means of establishing a more regulated administration. Non-Muslim prisoners taken in a new conquest were made to swear personal fealty to the Sultan and incorporated into the Janissary Corps or "New Army". The brightest of these new slaves were enrolled in the *devirsme*, or civil service, where they were converted to Islam, trained in the military arts, and educated in the role of civil administrators.[7] Murat also appointed a Grand Vizier to act as his chief minister to be responsible for the day-to-day operation of the civil government and military forces. This union of civil and military administration was mirrored at the district level as local governors were given authority over territories and administered a feudal system. The governor, or *Sanjak Bey*, was both an administrator and military leader responsible for overseeing farms in peace and organizing the cavalry in war.[8]

---

[5] McCarthey, *The Ottoman Turks,* 94.
[6] Ibid., 52.
[7] Ibid., 48.
[8] Bernard Lewis, *The Emergence of Modern Turkey*, 2nd ed. (Oxford: Oxford University Press, 1969), 384.

The military establishment formed the core of the Ottoman Empire and at the forefront of this organization was the Sultan's Janissary Corps. Drawn from the *ikta* system and loyal to the Sultan, the Janissaries formed the elite infantry backbone of the Army. They were well paid, disciplined and exceptionally loyal to the Sultan. A tenth of their number were trained and groomed for higher command. From 1453 to the late 1700s, every Grand Vizier, each provincial governor, as well as senior commanders were drawn from their ranks.[9] The Janissary Corps was the institution that allowed this system to exist, grow and thrive. Trained, educated, and equipped as an elite force, tribes and governors far from the capital city were compelled to respect this force's fighting efficiency. Order and the hierarchical control from Sultan to governor were maintained by the existence and periodic use of the Janissaries. This system functioned well as long as the Janissaries remained primarily focused on external threats, conquests and an occasional intervention in tribal affairs. The system dramatically changed when the Janissaries became a part of the empire's internal political dynamic. In the late 1500s, after the rule of Suleiman the Great, the Janissaries became much more proactive in advocating their political preferences by manipulating the lack of clear succession rules in the Sultan line. In the political vacuum caused by the death of a Sultan, the corps began to support their own candidates to the throne. In turn, the winning Sultans would repay their debt by increasing Janissary salaries and increasing their numbers. This became popularly known as the Sultan's "accession gift".[10] This tendency for military influence to override the administration of government created a lasting legacy very much in evidence today in the Turkish Republic.

Ottoman Legacy – Role of Islam

Ottoman rule was influenced by an additional and equally powerful factor; namely the Islamic faith. Conquests by the Sultan's armies were driven by the twin purposes of acquiring physical power and proselytizing the Islamic faith. The Ottomans were the first to adopt the Sharia as

[9] Christopher Houston, *Islam, Kurds and the Turkish Nation State* (Oxford: Berg, 2001), 3.

[10] McCarthey, *The Ottoman Turks*, 85.

their effective law and initialized it as the central basis of administration in their newly acquired land. A unique feature of these conquests was that conversion was never forced on their new subjects.[11] In strict observance of the Quran, conversion was voluntary. Consequently, other faith communities were divided into administrative units referred to as *millets* where their respective faith leaders became responsible for the education, welfare and personal law of its members. This tolerant policy proved pragmatic, since Christians and Jews made up sizeable portions of the empire as they expanded to traditionally non-Muslim lands. The Ottomans employed the church as a system of control while not alienating these subjects.[12] It was also clear that recognition of the *dhimmi* or "protected" symbolized a political inferiority.[13] The *dhimmi* conferred only tolerance and not equal consideration as Muslims under the law. Religion was not restricted as a mechanism of control over only non-Muslim subjects.

The Ottoman elite realized that the Sharia had its limitations when applied to the legal needs of administering an empire. Suleiman the Great, who ruled from 1520-1566, was the empire's greatest conqueror, but also its most astute administrator through his codification of administrative law. Historian Justin McCarthey opined that "most legal matters were the province of the Muslim religious law...but there was considerable scope for the Sultan's law, especially administrative law – matters of taxation, land tenure...Suleiman transformed the state into an organization of rules and set procedures, a feat as important in the long run as military conquests."[14] Suleiman sought to harmonize the administrative laws with the Islamic code. Turkish scholar Berdal Aral described this process as a concept called *din-ü-devlet* where there exists "a state governed by religion as well as religion in service of the state."[15] The ulema, in the employment of the state, was tasked to find justifications for administrative laws within the precepts of the Quran and Sharia. This balancing of

---

[11] Lewis, *The Emergence of Modern Turkey*, 11.

[12] McCarthey, *The Ottoman Turks*, 128.

[13] Richard Tapper, ed., *Islam in Modern Turkey* (London and New York: I. B. Taurus, 1991), 36.

[14] Tapper, ed., *Islam in Modern Turkey*, 87.

[15] Berdal Aral, "The Idea of Human Rights as Perceived in the Ottoman Empire," *Human Rights Quarterly* 26, no. 2 (May 2004): 465.

administrative need and religious mandate was a central component in the Empire's administration. Fundamental to understanding *din-u-devlet* was the concept of "tacit contract".

Islam posited that there existed a "tacit contract" between the people and the Sultan that results in a true Islamic order. The ruler could rule as long as he did not disregard the Holy law.[16] In the event the Sultan strayed, the people were empowered to take action and "this explains why, immediately after the outbreak of a revolt…the rebels made sure to incriminate the Sultan for breaching this tacit covenant, and accordingly, in case they achieved their goal, promised a 'return' to the proper, rightly guided state of the Islamic community."[17] This concept of the implicit authority to rule was difficult for a Western mind to grasp, but was essential in understanding the Ottoman Empire. Ottoman subjects obeyed their Sultan because his authority was derived from immutable religious law. The Sultan could only rule within the ideological confines of the Quran, Muhammad's sayings and authorized interpretations. Rights outside of this system did not exist. This tension between perceptions of religious and administrative needs and the right of just rule would manifest itself in several forms as the Ottoman Empire entered the 19th Century and came under the greater influence of the West.

Ottoman Legacy – Efforts to Reform

Ottoman military might was central to the empire's rise, but this reliance on the military instrument would also be its undoing. Throughout the 1600s, Ottoman military prowess declined and it was repeatedly challenged along its frontiers. As Europe flourished in the Renaissance period, the Ottoman court remained insular and content with its practices and methods of administration. This isolationist, if not arrogant, approach proved problematic as historian Justin McCarthey wrote "the Ottoman's might have been able to ignore European intellectual development if it had solely been a matter or art, literature and philosophy, but they could not ignore the presence of European armies at

---

[16] Aral, "The Idea of Human Rights as Perceived in the Ottoman Empire," 471.
[17] Ibid., 471.

their gates, armies made stronger than their own through technology."[18] The decline of the armed

forces then became both a sign of imperial decay and a cause of it. The Army was ill equipped to

fight and consequently lost battles. Losing battles pressured the civil authorities to seek ways to

improve their fighting efficiency in order to maintain the territorial integrity of the Empire. Reform

of the Empire, at least initially, focused on reforming the military and adopting the bureaucratic and

military structures and methods of their enemies.[19] Historians Dietrich Yung and Wolfgang Piccoli

termed the Ottoman efforts as "defensive modernization". Opening more direct contacts with

European powers and importing ideas had but one short term purpose; namely, preserve the

boundaries of the empire by mimicking the attributes of a modern army.[20] In 1711, Sultan Ahmed III

dispatched emissaries to the Courts of Europe to seek out new knowledge and practices and thus

began nearly 200 years of intermittent reforms based on European models. These reforms were not

readily embraced by much of the military establishment and particularly by the segment that truly

mattered, the Janissary Corps.

The Janissaries successfully limited the application of any reforms up through the 1820s

through brute force and intimidation. After centuries of building independent bases of power the

Janissary leadership was reluctant to adapt new techniques. Particularly troublesome to them was the

hierarchal command and control schemes and regimented drill that removed the individual warrior

aspect out of combat and replaced it with a more regimented organization.[21] The first direct

challenge to the Janissaries developed when Sultan Selim III formed a new body of troops fashioned

after the armies of revolutionary France in 1792. This *Nizam-i-Cedid* or "new ordered troops" were

proclaimed "un-Islamic" by the Janissaries in 1807 and were destroyed. Sultan Selim was also

---

[18] McCarthey, *The Ottoman Turks*, 148.
[19] Lewis, *The Emergence of Modern Turkey*, 2nd ed., 23-24.
[20] Dietrich Jung and Wolfgang Piccoli, *Turkey at the Crossroads* (London and New York: Zed Books, 2001), 39.
[21] McCarthey, *The Ottoman Turks*, 288.

ultimately deposed.[22] In 1826 Sultan Mahmud tried again to raise a modern regiment, but this time

arranged for a *fatwa* to be issued to support the modernization. In June 1827, when the Janissaries

moved to crush the new regiment, loyal troops and the local populous rose up to keep the Janissaries

in their barracks and then proceeded to exterminate the entire Janissary Corps.[23] Elimination of the

Janissaries proved to be the watershed event that opened the door to meaningful reform. It did not

diminish the influence of the military establishment on the political process. Beginning in the 1830s,

officers of the "new ordered" Army traveled even more extensively in Europe and returned with not

only a military education, but also with a profound exposure to Western ideas. Historian William

Hale claimed this class of "army officers saw themselves as the vanguard of reform and the

harbingers of enlightenment. Their educational system [staff colleges and European tours] separated

them from traditional society, sharpened their sense of corporate identity and political mission."[24]

The tension between military and civil control had taken on a new form. Where the Janissaries

sought to lessen the pace of reform and Westernization than pursued by the Sultan, the new order

sought its acceleration.

The period between 1840 and 1870 marked the period known as the *Tanzimat* ("those who

put things in order") reforms.[25] These reforms marked the true beginning of the end for the Ottoman

Empire. Failing to arrest the loss of territory to powers on their frontiers through simply military

transformation, the Sultans were compelled to seek out new solutions. Primary among these was a

perceived need to exert greater direct control over the outlying provinces and consolidation of power

within the central government structure. These efforts entailed ending the wide autonomy enjoyed by

the emirs, governors, and tribal leaders in the provinces. In order to break the regional holds on

power, the Sultans resolved to undermine the source of this power; land and taxation. The land code

of 1858 decreed all land would return to the ownership of the central government and then be

---

[22] Lewis, *The Emergence of Modern Turkey*, 2nd ed., 59.
[23] William Hale, *Turkish Politics and the Military* (New York: Routledge, 1994), 13.
[24] Hale, *Turkish Politics and the Military*, 54.
[25] McCarthey, *The Ottoman Turks*, 296.

redistributed to individuals. The law was intended to remove control from the hands of large landowners and entrust the land to those who actually tilled it. In reality, local tribal leaders, taking advantage of their education and knowledge of the law, simply reorganized their lands into their own private ownership.[26]

Another attempt at reform was the Reform Edict of 1856 which removed the defacto inequality between Muslim and Non-Muslim. The edict removed the special status of the *millets* from non-Muslims, which among other things, obligated non-Muslims to serve in the armed forces.[27] This completely redefined how subjects perceived their position in the empire. This alienation was compounded by the Sultan's attempts to open avenues for greater European influence in Ottoman political and economic structures. Soliciting foreign loans to finance modernization and integration into foreign markets, foreign investments were permitted for the first time in 1838. By 1854, the Empire was dependent on foreign capital and was bankrupt by 1870. In 1875, the Ottomans agreed to "Capitulations" where European were granted supranational status and empowered to control imperial finances to repay foreign debt.[28] The sum of these changes challenged the "tacit contract" and put into question the true nature of the relationship between the Sultan and Allah. *Tanzimat* was to put things in order, but the more practical observation was that it reordered the political landscape in a manner foreign to many subjects.

The consternation caused by these dramatic changes forced many, particularly the intelligentsia, to re-evaluate the course of the Ottoman Empire. It appeared to some that the identity of the Empire was fragmenting as old ways and territories were stripped away. In 1865, a group of intellectuals formed a group called the Young Ottomans and pursued a course that focused on the emergence of a Turkish identity to supplant the traditional, totalitarian and Islamic authority of the

---

[26] Martin van Bruissen, *Agah, Shaikh and State* (London and New Jersey: Zed Books, 1992), 182-183.
[27] Aral, "The Idea of Human Rights as Perceived in the Ottoman Empire," 478.
[28] Dietrich Jung and Wolfgang Piccoli, *Turkey at the Crossroads*, 42.

Ottoman Empire.[29] In 1877, this group managed to convince Sultan Abdulhamid to create a constitution and establish a parliament. The Sultan, pressured by persistent military threats, the Capitulations regime, and not able to compel greater control of the provinces, saw few other options.[30] In March 1877, this parliament convened for the first time. The Sultan could not deal with its openness, and the voice it gave to opposition, so he terminated its short life in June of the same year. The Young Ottomans did not have the full support or complicity of the one, true power broker in the Ottoman Empire, that being the Army. The Young Turks would not suffer this handicap.

The Young Turks were formed in 1889 by four medical students, two of whom were Kurdish. The Young Turks advocated the formation of a Turkish state based on the foundations of Turkish nationalism and identity. This was the only means by which to stop the disintegration of the empire by holding on to its ethnically trusted core. The essential differentiating characteristic between the Young Ottomans and the Young Turks was the support of the military elite. The officer corps was increasingly dissatisfied with the continuing military reverses and the growing foreign encroachment in the administration of the Empire. These officers were armed with the broader education provided by the military reforms and became the vanguard of the Young Turk movement. This provided the Young Turks with what their predecessors lacked, a broader appeal backed by the force of arms.[31] The Officer Corps would quickly become the organization's center of gravity and in 1908 staged a "coup" that introduced the Committee for Unity and Progress (CUP) as the executive authority operating under the nominal rule of the Sultan. A parliament was introduced and by March 1909 the CUP exercised direct control, regulating the Sultan to near figurehead status. The new Republic was now in an embryonic stage, but it would still require 16 more years to develop.

[29] Lewis, *The Emergence of Modern Turkey*, 2nd ed., 153.
[30] McCarthey, *The Ottoman Turks*, 300.
[31] Lewis, *The Emergence of Modern Turkey*, 2nd ed., 197.

Effects of the Ottoman Legacy

There were four enduring features of the Ottoman Empire that continue to impact on the modern Turkish state. These were: (1) the perceived need for strong central control, (2) the use of Islam as a control mechanism, and (3) the primacy of the military in political affairs. From the time Osman exerted greater influence over his fellow tribal chiefs to become the central authority, Ottoman administration was based on the creation of new arrangements to hold together a confederation of different tribes, cultures and religions. In most instances, some form of coercion was required to meet this objective. Adaptation of the *ikta* to consolidate this rule and enforce it was instrumental to the process. When coercion fell short, the Sultan relied on the precepts of the Islamic faith to keep the polity at least functionally loyal to the center. Unity in faith helped create the empire and adaptation of the faith's strictures helped to stabilize it. Suleiman's expansion on the *din-ü-devlet* created a self-reinforcing principle that the state serves the faith while the faith supports the state. Islam was the social anchor to the entire system. Even the *dhimmi* helped control the population by allowing minority groupings to govern themselves within the limits set forth by the empire.

The most enduring of the Ottoman legacies was the relation of the military to the state. From the Janissaries to the Committee on Unity and Progress, the armed forces in the Ottoman tradition played the role of final arbiter of political power. Initially created to protect the central power, the practice of integrating the military into the political framework led to usurpation of civil rule. The *devirsme* tradition produced a corps of officers much better educated and with a more cosmopolitan view of the world than the average citizen and even the royal line. Greater exposure to the West through attendance at European military colleges only increased this level of awareness. Education and awareness, when coupled with the need for state defense or survival provided sufficient motivation to the officer corps to become politically active. Similar to the reinforcing state and religion paradigm, the use of the military to lead the reform effort eventually abdicated control of the process to the intellectually enlightened military elite. Reform of the empire equated to military reform and institutions were redesigned along those martial lines. Military intervention in the conduct of state administration became an accepted norm.

CHAPTER THREE

Kemalism – Mustafa Kemal and the New Republic

On October 29, 1918, the Ottomans signed the Armistice with the victorious Western powers and so concluded the painful experience of the First World War for the Ottoman Empire. The Ottomans were drawn into the war and had supported Germany in hope of gaining a powerful patron to obtain assistance for a modernization program while simultaneously protecting its territory from Russian aggression. This decision by the Committee on Unity and Progress (CUP) to go to war on the side of Germany only hastened the disintegration of empire. Allied intentions to dismember the Ottoman Empire were clear. The post-war plans allocated large portions of Anatolia to the Greeks, reserved both an Armenian and Kurdish enclave in the east, and divided the remainder of the empire to French and British spheres of influence. With the Young Turks and CUP discredited in the war, Sultan Abdulhamid saw an opportunity to cling to at least a portion of Anatolia. As Allied forces entered Istanbul in February 1919, the Sultan made the most of this opportunity and eliminated the last vestiges of the Young Turks and the CUP in an effort to reassert the monarchy and order. The war leadership of the CUP was discredited, but the post-war power vacuum created opportunities for other reformers. Large portions of Ottoman territory remained unoccupied by the Allies and remained under the control of reform minded officers. While the Allied Powers occupied Istanbul and dealt with the Sultan, the reformers in the provinces bided their time for an opportunity.[32]

The prime catalyst for action was the introduction of a historic and bitter enemy. When the Greek Army landed in eastern Anatolia in May of 1919, the population became energized and began to re-rally around the Young Turks and its military vanguard. The task of leading this new nationalist movement fell to Mustafa Kemal, a hero of Gallipoli and the only true Turkish military hero of the First World War. Under his leadership, a resistance to the foreign occupation coalesced. In July of 1919, Kemal resigned his commission and established an alternate, nationalist powerbase in Ankara

---

[32] Dietrich Jung and Wolfgang Piccoli, *Turkey at the Crossroads* (London and New York: Zed Books, 2001), 67.

which competed in the December 1919 elections and subsequently won a majority in parliament. In April 1920, the Sultan dissolved the parliament and encouraged the issuance of a *fatwa* condemning the Kemalist movement. Just as it appeared that the Kemalists would be marginalized and the Sultan able to consolidate his power, the completion of the Treaty of Sevres in June of 1920 dramatically altered the conditions.

The Treaty of Sevres was to be the final peace agreement between the Allies and Ottoman Empire. The provisions of the treaty dismembered portions of the Empire, allocating large portions to Allied control and Armenian and Kurdish autonomy. This attack on the territorial integrity coupled with Kemal's victories over the Greeks in 1921 and 1922 spurred on nationalist feelings and drove many into the Kemalist camp[33]. Riding this wave of success and popularity, Kemal was able to complete the defeat of the Greeks and prevented the Allies from imposing the conditions of Sevres. In 1922, the Treaty of Sevres was replaced with the Treaty of Lausanne which created the modern boundaries of the Turkish state and preserved what was termed the historical lands of the Turks.[34] In November of 1922, Kemal eliminated the Sultanate and made Ankara the new seat of government.

Mustafa Kemal, later to be known as Kemal Ataturk or "Father of the Turks", laid the foundations of the modern Turkish state. His six principles of "Kemalism"; republicanism, secularism, nationalism, populism, statism and revolutionism, form the core of the Turkish state and was the lens through which modern Turk policymakers viewed themselves and the world.[35] An important attribute not explicitly iterated by Ataturk, but what has become common practice and subsequently enshrined in later constitutions, was the assertion that "the military has both the right and the responsibility to intervene in affairs of state, when absolutely necessary in order to guarantee the system's continuance."[36] Ataturk's brand of nationalism, the "six arrows" of Kemalism and the military tradition, was both a result and continuation of Ottoman reforms to bring the Turks into the

---

[33] Lewis, *The Emergence of Modern Turkey*, 2nd ed., 252.
[34] Paul White, *Primitive Rebels or Revolutionary Modernizers?* (New York: Zed Books, 2000), 70.
[35] Michael M. Gunter, *The Kurds and the Future of Turkey* (New York: St. Martin's, 1997), 6.
[36] White, *Primitive Rebels or Revolutionary Modernizers?*, 130.

modern age.[37] Ataturk's approach emphasized the need of keeping the Turkish state within balance. He advocated a state that retained its nationalist identity, made efforts to Westernize and modernize, and kept Islamic traditions in equilibrium. Failure to maintain this delicate balance would make the republic susceptible to the ills of the Ottomans: weakness due to cultural fragmentation, suspicion of new ways, and religious superstition. His efforts were initially focused on the process of secularization.

Kemalism – Ataturk and Secularization

Two years after the elimination of the Sultanate, the new Turkish Republic similarly dissolved the greatest symbol of the Islamic Ottoman Empire, the Caliphate. Ataturk justified the move by emphasizing what Bernard Lewis states as "three main points: the safeguarding and stabilization of the Republic, the creation of a unified national system of education, and the need to cleanse and elevate the Islamic faith by rescuing it from the position of a political instrument."[38] Ataturk could not allow Islam to impede Kemalism by distorting the process of modern education and limiting the alternatives to modernization by "superstition" and antiquated thought. Turkish political scientists Metin Heper and Aylin Guney posit that the educated elites, which formed the vanguard of Kemalism, "equated Islam with irrationality…they perceived a close relationship between the demise of the Ottoman Empire and the persistent opposition of religion to the modernization efforts of the late eighteenth and early part of the nineteenth centuries."[39] The Republic also realized that it could not completely eliminate religion as a factor as the practice of Islam was in the very fiber of society. This loyalty to Islam could only be reordered and not completely supplanted. Much like Suleiman, Ataturk incorporated the faith into the official apparatus of the government.

---

[37] Gunter, *The Kurds and the Future of Turkey*, 6.
[38] Lewis, *The Emergence of Modern Turkey*, 2nd ed., 264.
[39] Metin Heper and Aylin Guney, "The Military and the Consolidation of Democracy: The Recent Turkish Experience," *Armed Forces and Society* 26, no. 4 (Summer 2000): 636.

Islamic scholar Ziya Gokalp formed the intellectual underpinnings of Ataturk's secularization program. Gokalp suggested that the Quran and sayings of Mohammed were constructed in the specific social context of their day. Gokalp argued that the rules derived during the days of Mohammed needed to be updated to meet current contextual realities.[40] One of Ataturk's first steps at diminishing the structural controls of Islam on society was the creation of the Department of Religious Affairs. This agency was the sole government agency to incorporate the functions of religion. He subsequently dismantled state sponsored religious schools and outlawed religiously based political parties. The state, through the Department of Religious Affairs, allowed, encouraged and even organized Islamic assemblies, but its control of the content of these functions denuded these functions of political content. Historian Christopher Houston commented "clearly perceiving itself as imbued with the task of constructing civil Islam with the civil strand of Kemalism, official Islam is in fact unable to criticize Turkish nationalism's ethnic preference without simultaneously de-legitimizing its own existence. For bureaucratized Islam is integral to the Kemalist project of subordinating notions of identity derived from Islam to one derived from the nation."[41] Kemalism also rejected the *millet* system as contrary to the nationalist ideal. Turkishness thus became the overarching unifier as opposed to Islam with specified, ethno-religious caveats. This subordination has not been completed, and the tension it created often percolated to the surface. The battle between Islam and secularism remained a defining characteristic of the Turk Republic.

Kemalism – Westernization and Reform

While the secularization program redefined perceptions of citizenship and nationalism as being separate from Islam, Ataturk also sought to pull the state towards modernity. Ataturk equated modernization with Westernization. In order to modernize, he understood that the pull of nationalism and Islam would still color popular perceptions of modernization. These influences would effect

---

[40] C. H. Dodd, *Democracy and Development in Turkey* (Northgate: Eothen Press, 1979), 81.
[41] Houston, *Islam, Kurds and the Turkish Nation State*, 90.

what the citizens would accept.[42] Ataturk created the Republican People's Party (RPP) as the mechanism to control this debate as the single ruling party. This arrangement lasted until his death when, in 1946, internal party wrangling caused a split. The splinter group formed the Democratic Party and began to gather other disaffected elements of the electorate under its banner.[43] This political liberalization ran parallel to a post World War II economic boom. When growth slowed in the late 1950s, the political situation soured and popular discontent came to be displayed in the proliferation of political parties.[44] The liberalization of the electorate then had a dual and often conflicting impact. It first placated the popular demand for political expression, but as conditions worsened, enabled the emergence of strong and increasingly violent government opposition. Greater political voice coupled with exposure to the market forces of a newly opened economy produced severe political turbulence.

As the country plunged into internal turmoil external influences intervened. Due to its strategic position in relation to the Soviet Union, Turkey was courted by the United States and the North Atlantic Treaty Organization (NATO) to act as a buffer and deterrent on Europe's southern flank. NATO's attention brought with it a great influx of US equipment and training and radically enhanced the proficiency of Turkish armed forces. Greater power also brought greater influence to the military high command. This influence would be exerted domestically to bring order back to the escalating chaos. Sensing that the political pluralism, though a necessary element of Westernization, could undermine its relationship with NATO, the Turkish military resolved to fulfill its traditional role. It would move to preserve the Republic.

In response to the widespread violence, a military junta seized power in May 1960. This marked the first of four military coups that was to define Turkish politics for the next forty years. The National Unity Committee (NUC) assumed control of all governmental functions and was widely

---

[42] Ilter Turan, "Religion and Political Culture in Turkey," in *Islam in Modern Turkey*, ed. Richard Tapper (London and New York: I. B. Taurus and Company, 1991), 46.

[43] David McDowell, *A Modern History of the Kurds*, 3rd ed. (New York: St. Martin's, 2005), 397.

[44] Tapper, *Islam in Modern Turkey*, 6.

accepted.[45] The NUC went on to draft a Constitution and, in so doing, codified the Military's future role in Turkish government. Principle among these inclusions was subordination of the Chief of the General Staff only to the Prime Minister (vice the Minister of Defense) and creation of the National Security Council (MGK). The MGK was a civilian and military body comprised of cabinet officials, Chief of the General Staff and serving force commanders. Its primary focus was national security issues, but was granted wide authority on economic and social policy and was given virtual veto authority on all government policy.[46] The NUC transferred power back to civil authorities after elections held in October 1961 with its interests safely preserved in the body of the MGK. Unfortunately for the military leadership, this course correction did not produce the intended long term effects.

A series of weak coalition governments prompted the military to act again in 1971. This coup, commonly referred to as "the coup by memorandum", was initiated by a letter sent to the government leadership to create a "credible" government or face an immediate armed revolt by military forces.[47] The civilian leadership complied, but the continuing partisan politics could not impose law and order on the increasingly unstable populous. In 1980, the military intervened directly and assumed direct control and ruled the country through the MGK. After a comprehensive law and order campaign waged by Turkish security forces and the abolishment of some political parties, the MGK transitioned authority back to civil control after elections in 1983. Military intervention was not complete. In its final intervention, the military establishment was to directly address the role of Islam in the political process.

The MGK and military establishment was quite content with the resulting order produced by the 1980 coup, at least initially. The civilian governments that followed were unable to manage the troubled economy and popular discontent associated with it. The mid-1980s saw the emergence of

---

[45] Hale, *Turkish Politics and the Military*, 122.
[46] Ibid., 138.
[47] Ibid., 184.

armed civil unrest highlighted by the rise of the PKK. While the military turned its attention to the PKK civilian coalition governments muddled on. Conditions improved in the mid-1990s with some measurable success against the PKK and a rebounding economy, but political instability persisted. In June of 1996, a coalition government was formed between the Refah Party, an Islamic oriented party, and the True Path Party. Necmeitin Erbakan of the Refah Party became Prime Minister while Tansu Ciller of the True Path acted as his deputy. These two parties were able to come to power as a result of popular backlash against a series of corruption scandals in government.[48] The Refah proved adept at organizing at the grassroots level and also often acted as a social welfare agency, emphasizing its Islamic roots. It therefore commanded a great degree of local support.

Erbakan and the Refah initiated quite radical policy moves by enforcing the construction of Muslim chapels in all embassies and commissioning all Ambassadors to be missionaries for Islam.[49] In February of 1997, local Refah commissioners in the city of Sincan staged a pro-Palestinian rally.[50] Prime Minister Erbakan reinforced these activities by visiting fundamentalist Islamic states such as Libya and Iran and issuing favorable statements about their relations with Turkey. These overt sympathies for political Islam greatly concerned the military members of the MGK and precipitated a statement declaring political Islam the top national security threat to the nation in January 1997. In February 1997 the MGK issued 18 recommendations to the government to get it back on the secular path. When these requests were ignored, the military began organizing mass protest rallies in April of that year. In a bizarre case of miscues, Deputy Prime Minister Ciller convinced Erbakan to resign his post in a complicated effort to switch posts and thus partly mollify the military. Erbakan complied, but in an unexpected master stroke, moderate President Suleyman Demirel selected a moderate, Mesut Yilmay to the post with the mandate to reform the government. In January 1998, the

---

[48] Heper and Guney, "The Military and the Consolidation of Democracy: The Recent Turkish Experience" 637.
[49] Ibid., 641.
[50] Ibid., 642.

Constitutional Court dissolved the Refah Party on the grounds that it had attempted to establish a state based on Islam.[51] The MGK had indirectly staged its fourth coup.

Kemalism – Effects

Kemalism produced two enduring and inter-related features within the new Turkish Republic. First, the Republic's leadership realized that the balance between nationalist identity, secularism and modernization required frequent and uncompromising interventions to maintain it. Only through a central authority could the political process be confined within acceptable limits.[52] The mechanism for enforcement of these boundaries, and second enduring feature of Kemalism, was the Turkish military. Intervention by the armed forces in politics and governance was enshrined in public law and generally accepted as part and parcel of Turkish civil practice. Civilian politicians and administrators were continually faced with the challenge of keeping dialogue and policy within the allowed tolerance. The tough questions and free competition inherent in liberal democracies were pushed aside for the sake of unity and order. Modernization and reform, and the disaffected citizens this process naturally created, were then a closely regulated by-product and not open to a free-flowing debate and critical examination of options. The entire political debate was forced to take place within the rational environs of secularism. Religious questions, though historically a part of the people's identity, were segregated and minimized. The Kemalist legacies limited options and defined what true progress consisted of and how national objectives were to be met.

---

[51]Heper and Guney, "The Military and the Consolidation of Democracy: The Recent Turkish Experience" 644.

[52] Jung and Piccoli, *Turkey at the Crossroads*, 62.

CHAPTER FOUR

International Context

An analysis of the Turkish Construct is not complete without examining the international context within which it operates. In the case of Turkey and its efforts against the PKK, the understanding of context is essential to comprehension of the conflict's meaning. Many different parties, including state, non-state and transnational organizations have an interest in its outcome and influenced the situation in some manner. The resulting external pressures have stressed all elements of the construct forcing Turkey to make hard choices to keep it on the Kemalist path. The desire to westernize played the largest role in making decisions about its external environment, but Islam and nationalism also factored heavily, particularly in how the Republic dealt with its immediate neighbors. Turkey is a strategically important state sitting on the vital crossroads between Europe, Asia and the Middle East. Geographically and ideologically, it resides in a highly contentious locale. Turkey's war with the PKK has become much more than an internal problem of quelling a dissident group. It has become a battleground for proxy wars between competing geopolitical interests. There are just as many powerful parties that wished Turkey to succeed as there were parties that wished it to fail.

International Context – Regional Actors

Turkey's immediate neighbors of Iran, Syria and Iraq have done the most to undermine the Turkish responses to the PKK insurgency. Through direct support of PKK actions by such means as direct financing and the provision of sanctuary, the PKK acted as the proxy of these states to further their own interests at the expense of Turkey. All three of these states were concerned with primarily their own Kurdish populations and what Kurdish autonomy would mean, maintaining a local balance of power in their favor, and containing the pro-western influences evident in the Turkish state.

Iranian interests were centered on keeping Turkish ambitions in the Trans-Caucuses in check, and preventing the expansion of western ways farther into the Middle East. Both the PKK and Iraqi

Kurds benefited from Iranian sanctuaries along with their financial support and provision of critically needed materiel to prosecute their guerilla war. Believing that Turkey was instrumental in funding the Mojahedin-e Khalq (MEK), a paramilitary movement residing in Iraqi territory committed to re-establishing a non-fundamentalist regime in Tehran, supporting the PKK acted as a form of retribution.[53] The collapse of the Soviet Union also placed Ankara and Tehran in competition to win influence in the newly independent Caucuses. Iranian policies towards these ends were not without its contradictions. Desiring to keep its own Kurds firmly under their rule, full Kurdish independence was not their objective. The aim of this policy was essentially a negative one. Though not desirous of a PKK victory, internal agitation would keep the Turkish state off-balance and focused away from Iranian interests.[54]

Syrian support had similarly negative aims and was much more overt. Without Syrian complicity, the PKK would not have been able to establish its political and logistical base so effectively. Ideologically, Syrian and Iranian interests shared the notion that Turkish cultural influences, tainted by western exposure, were to be contained. Syrian motivations were also much more pragmatic. Traditionally, Syria and Turkey have squabbled over water rights, as the headwaters of the Euphrates are controlled by Turkey, which potentially leaves Syrian and Iraqi access to water at Turkey's mercy.[55] Destabilization of Turkey and keeping it weak became President Assad's aim when he agreed to shelter the PKK within its territory and the Lebanese Baca valley.[56] With its own Kurdish population well in hand, Syria had greater latitude in how hard it pushed the Turks.

Iraq's position in the conflict is a complicated one as it has both hindered and helped each side of the conflict. Kurdish activism in Iraq and Saddam Hussein's inability to completely suppress the Kurdish uprisings created a de-facto Kurdish enclave on Turkey's southern border. In April 1979,

---

[53] Michael M. Gunter, *The Kurds and the Future of Turkey*, 95.
[54] Ibid., 95.
[55] Michael Radu, ed., in *Dangerous Neighborhood*, (New Brunswick: Transaction, 2003), 14.
[56] Steven J. Blank, Stephen C. Pelletier, and William T. Johnsen, *Turkey's Strategic Position at the Crossroads of World Affairs* (Carlisle: Strategic Studies Institute, 1993), 35.

Turkey entered into agreement with Baghdad that called for military cooperation along the border to suppress the movement and militant activities of all Kurdish groups in the area. In 1984, this agreement was expanded to include hot-pursuit provisions. Saddam went as far as conceding control of a buffer area to the Turkish government while his attention was diverted on the Iran-Iraq war.[57] Meanwhile, in order to exploit the advantage of the proximity of their Iraqi Kurd cousins, the PKK concluded an alliance with the Kurdistan Democratic Party (KDP). Kurdish alliances proved short-lived for two reasons. Turkey cross border operations increasingly inflicted casualties on the KDP and fellow Iraqi Kurdish group the Patriotic Union of Kurdistan (PUK). Additionally, PKK tactics employed within Turkey alienated the Iraqi Kurd leadership. By 1987, the KDP disavowed its relationship with the PKK and joined PUK forces in combating PKK camps within Iraqi territory. The PKK can be attributed with helping the rapprochement between the KDP and PUK. Faced with several common enemies; Turkey, Iraq and the PKK backed by Syria and Iran, the two Iraqi Kurd groups were compelled to cooperate for survival. The resiliency of the Iraqi Kurds proved to be a major issue in the development of the larger, regional Kurdish issue particularly with Operations Desert Storm, Provide Comfort and Iraqi Freedom.

Regional actors played a key role in prolonging the conflict and encouraging progression towards what counter-insurgency expert C. E. Caldwell's terms a desultory form of conflict. Strengths and weaknesses on both sides were countermanded by complementary strength and weaknesses on the other side. Syrian support kept the PKK position viable, but was not sufficient to defeat the Turkish Army. Iranian complicity provided much of the same kind of limited support. Neither provision proved decisive. Iraqi Kurdistan and cooperation of Saddam Hussein presented possibilities for both sides, but one offset the other. The PKK could not sustain the support of the KDP nor the PUK while Saddam's inability to crush his Kurdish minority kept the enclave, defacto

[57] Philip Robins, "The Overlord State: Turkish Policy and the Kurdish Issue," *International Affairs* 69, no. 4 (October 1993), 672.

sanctuary, and subsequent PKK hopes alive. These complex regional inter-relationships and varying allegiances also played themselves out in the greater international context.

Israel proved to be the one cooperative neighbor for Turkey. In an unlikely marriage of interests between the Jewish state and once epitome of Islamic rule, both states worked together to forge a political and military cooperative in 1992. These ties were fashioned largely as an effort to offset their common enemy, Syria. For Turkey, Israel was a reliable supplier of arms and did not tie sales of these arms to human rights. Middle East scholar Efraim Inbar noted "This partnership is characteristic of two satisfied (non-revisionist) powers cooperating primarily to preserve the regional status quo and to fend off common threats."[58]

International Context – Western Influence

The Cold War vaulted Turkey into a prominent position on the world stage. The North Atlantic Treaty Organization (NATO) perceived Turkey as a critical line of defense against Soviet hegemony into southern Europe and the Middle East. Turkey's strategic location made it invaluable to the Western Alliance and was accepted into NATO. The protection and status afforded by NATO membership produced a series of internal changes. Stephen Larrabee writes that "in many ways the Cold War arrested Turkey's evolution by legitimizing the special role of the military in Turkish politics and reinforcing its preference for controlled or guided democracy. At the same time it made it easier to suppress certain political forces, particularly Islam and Kurdish nationalism."[59] The demise of the Soviet Union did not diminish Turkey's importance to the Western world, but may have augmented it. It remained a state astride three turbulent state entities: Iran, Syria and Iraq.[60] One substantial difference, one that fundamentally changed the character of Turkey's relationship with the rest of the world, was that Turkey's internal practices became a source of contention. The world's

---

[58] Afrain Inbar, "Turkey's New Strategic Partner Israel," in *Dangerous Neighborhood*, ed. Michael Radu (New Brunswick: Transaction, 2003), 171.

[59] Stephen Larrabee, "US and European Policy Towards Turkey and the Caspian Basin," in *Allies Divided,* ed. Robert Blackwell and Michael Sturmer (Cambridge: MIT Press, 1997), 165.

[60] Blank, Pelletier, and Johnsen, *Turkey's Strategic Position at the Crossroads of World Affairs,* 2.

scrutiny of Turkish governance, once averted to avoid conflict with Cold War security imperatives, was now fully on Turkey as the Berlin Wall collapsed. It was no longer enough to be an ally on the ideological fault line. Current conditions and external perceptions often placed Turkey in a contradictory and untenable position. Its sometimes autocratic government, bureaucracy, and centralized economy make it frequently unattractive to the Western audience while its secularism and western ties make it equally repugnant to the east.[61] In order to pursue its international and domestic goals under the glare of world attention, the Turkish state has been forced to adopt creative solutions and make the most of opportunities.

Operations Desert Storm and Provide Comfort offered two such opportunities. Joining the US led coalition in the First Gulf War against Saddam Hussein legitimized Turkey's position and granted it greater latitude in controlling its southern border. Participating in this endeavor was no small decision as it countermanded a Kemalist principle of not unduly provoking a neighbor in a direct confrontation.[62] The eviction of Saddam from Kuwait also brought much more than bargained for. Saddam's immediate and brutal response to the ensuing Kurd and Shia uprisings forced many Kurds to flee across the border into Turkey. This presented a massive humanitarian problem with Turkey at center stage, where it was in a position to alleviate the suffering and take action. Still mindful of the many advantages to be accrued from backing the US policy in the region, Turkey became a critical component in both the protection of the Iraqi Kurds via humanitarian assistance, protecting the refugees from Iraqi pursuit, and later basing aircraft in support of Operation Northern Watch. In regards to the Kurds and execution of US policy, Turkey became the indispensable ally.

Provide Comfort also offered some advantage to the PKK. The media coverage of the entire Kurdish issue and public attention on the debate of Kurdish identity gave the PKK cause a boost. The PKK sought to capitalize on the international sympathy for Iraqi Kurds by propagating the greater Kurdish cause. The PKK cause was materially aided by the eventual withdrawal of Saddam's forces

---

[61] Blank, Pelletier, and Johnsen, *Turkey's Strategic Position at the Crossroads of World Affairs*, 14.
[62] Ibid., 39.

from northern Iraq as the Iraqi Kurds began the administration of an autonomous region. The renewal of in-fighting between the PUK and KDP, which occurred in the mid-1990s, added further cover to PKK operations in the quasi-sanctuary of Northern Iraq. This instability was not entirely advantageous as Turkey used the turmoil as grounds for more military incursions into Iraq. Controlling the vital communications and supply link between the KDP and PUK to the outside world, the Turkish Army exerted a great deal of pressure on these groups. Control of the border and sometimes inhospitable treatment by its KDP and PUK hosts limited the usefulness of this PKK sanctuary. Ultimately, Desert Storm and Provide Comfort provided very little material support to the PKK while providing the Turkish military better positions and much more attentive Western patrons for its war against the PKK. What the PKK was able to capitalize on, and to the detriment of the Turkish government, was the exposure now granted to the Kurdish problem. How the Turkish government treated its Kurds now became a substantial impediment to the Turkish desire for moving closer to the West and integration into the European Union (EU).

EU integration has long been a goal for Turkish policymakers. Stephen Larrabee concludes that "Ankara has seen full membership in the EU as a symbol of the successful completion of the Ataturk revolution."[63] The drive to make this a reality has caused the Turkish government to make substantial compromises and EU policies had a direct impact on Turkish governance, including the methods its used to prosecute the war against the PKK. Strategic positioning was not enough to convince the EU that Turkey should be admitted. Turkish selling points included portraying itself as a stabilizing force on Europe's periphery and as the corridor for energy resources flowing into Europe from the Caspian Sea and Central Asia.[64] Europe's attention was not on security or economics, but rather on Human Rights and how they were applied to its Kurdish minority. The PKK also used its own European connections to its advantage. There were an estimated 500,000 Kurds throughout

---

[63] Larrabee, "US and European Policy Towards Turkey and the Caspian Basin," 159.
[64] Inbar, "Turkey's New Strategic Partner: Israel,", 167.

Western Europe.[65] These Kurds have been a source of funding through remittances and a conduit to lobby European governments.

In 1997, in a response to the gradual development of former Warsaw Bloc states, the EU began the process of granting membership to some of these states. In doing so, they completely ignored Turkey's application submitted since 1987. Ankara suspended relations with the EU, but reopened them when the EU decided to consider them as other candidate states, due largely to the insistence of the United States. The primary stumbling block to progression of their application became adherence to the Copenhagen Criteria that requires states to have stable institutions, have a solid basis in the rule of law, and uphold human rights and protect minorities. Since 2001, Turkey implemented seven reform packages or "Harmonization Laws" to meet EU demands.[66] In an effort to establish the baseline of EU human rights requirements, Turkey became a party to several human rights conventions. Most notable of these was the European Convention of Human Rights which incorporates the European Court of Human Rights (EHCR) as a binding judicial body on municipal law. Aslan Gunduz remarked that "hardly any other country in the world has been criticized for its human rights record, nor is the future of any other country so dependent on the promotion of human rights …the EHCR exercises a decisive, if indirect influence on the Turkish legal and political system."[67] Provisions of the convention allowed Turkish citizens to bring cases before the EHCR if all local remedies were exhausted. From November 1998, when Turkey ratified the convention, to June 2000, 2,500 petitions had gone to the EHCR from Turkey. In these cases the EHCR largely ignored the local remedy rule and often acted as a court of first instance.[68]

The Human Rights issue presented a quandary. The Turkish government was required to satisfy its internal need for security while simultaneously compelled to adhere to a series of acts it felt

---

[65] Robbins, "The Overlord State: Turkish Policy and the Kurdish Issue," 663.

[66] Robbins, "The Overlord State: Turkish Policy and the Kurdish Issue," 663.

[67] Aslan Gunduz, "Turkey and Europe: The Human Rights Conundrum," in *Dangerous Neighborhood,* ed. Michael S. Radu, (New Brunswick: Transaction, 2003), 26.

[68] Ibid., 29.

jeopardized the effective prosecution of its counter-insurgency campaign. Alternatively, the EU provided the potential access to resources desperately needed to revitalize the Turkish economy and rebuild the devastated Kurdish regions. Direct negotiations to admit Turkey into the European Union began in October 2005 after a long and bitter process. Whether Turkey is finally admitted is still very much in doubt. As recently as November 2005, EU officials castigated the Turkish delegation for "no progress at all" in the development of the southeast.[69] Some members of the EU perceive Turkey as a danger to the social and cultural unity of the continent while most accept that Turkey does represent a buffer of sorts with the unstable Middle East. The pressing security issues on Europe's southern borders and active lobbying by the United States have allowed the Turkish candidacy to remain alive.

The US has been Turkey's main supporter on its three core issues: EU membership, the Caspian oil line, and the PKK.[70] Turkey is supported as a main line of defense against Islamic extremism and as a model for a democratic Middle East may look like. Turkey has continued to exhibit its bona fides by its support for the Global War on Terror (GWOT). It was the only Muslim nation to join the US action in Afghanistan under the auspices of NATO. Though Turkish public opinion was 80% against committing Turkish forces, Prime Minister Bulent Ecevit "justified his government's decision by noting that having fought terrorism for so long [against the PKK] Turkey would have denied itself if it chose to opt out of this war."[71] Maintaining a close relationship with the US has somewhat mitigated the effects of the problems experienced with the EU. Cloaking the PKK under the auspices of the GWOT, the Turkish government has added a degree of legitimacy to its efforts.

International considerations cannot be divorced from an analysis of the Turkish-PKK struggle. Both sides attempted to leverage an advantage from the geopolitical realities that surround

---

[69] Speech of Olli Rehn to EU-Turkey Joint Parliamentary Committee, 23 November 2005, *Brussels Rapid Database*, Brussels.
[70] Larrabee, "US and European Policy Towards Turkey and the Caspian Basin," 152.
[71] Birol A. Yesilada, "Turkish-US Relations," in *Dangerous Neighborhood*, ed. Michael S. Radu (New Brunswick: Transaction, 2003), 193.

the conflict. No decisive relationship has been formed by this international outreach. The effect of such international influence appears to have only prolonged the conflict by granting each side access to greater resources. This has proven a far greater detriment to the Turkish cause than to the PKK. Obvious external threats from Iran, Syria, and Iraq only legitimized military supremacy over policy. Threats to national security and territorial integrity of the state justified repressive measures and muted alternative voices. On the other side of the international support balance sheet was the fact that international attention kept the Kurdish question in the world's consciousness. Though the PKK was branded a terrorist organization, the privations of the Kurdish people remained a source for sympathy.

CHAPTER FIVE

Kurds and the Turkish Construct

The Kurdish threat to the Turkish state has existed since the inception of the Republic.

Though initially tolerant of Kurdish autonomy in principle, Ataturk soon resolved that no divergence

from a pure Turkish identity could be tolerated.[72] The "Kurdish Question", as it has been frequently

referred to, struck right at the heart of the Turkish state because the issue was intertwined with all four

components of the Turkish Construct. A Kurdish identity was contrary to Ataturk's brand of

nationalism. Similarly, the Kurds' more pious orientation in regards to Islam presented an added

challenge to secularism and their rural/pastoral conditions were an affront to

modernization/Westernization. All of these differences with Kemalism were in stark contrast to the

position enjoyed by the Kurds in the Ottoman Empire. Within the Empire, the Sultans allotted the

Kurds a great deal of autonomy for two basic reasons. They resided in relatively inaccessible terrain

and provided a great service to the Empire by protecting the eastern frontier from Persians, Russians,

and Armenians.[73] The Kemalist revolution marked a clear break from the historical position enjoyed

by the Kurds in the Ottoman Empire.

The Kurdish people have often been considered the largest ethnic group without a state.[74]

This historical interpretation inferred a degree of cultural homogeneity that did not exist. Kurdish

expert Michael Gunter suggested two principal stumbling blocks existed to a national Kurdish

identity. The first impediment was language as three major dialects, and two minor ones, were found

in three large areas of Kurdistan and all are virtually unintelligible from one another. The second

obstacle was a strong tradition of tribalism. The institutions of *agah* (feudal landlord or tribal

chieften) and *sheikhs* (religious leader of an Islamic sect) gained power throughout the Ottoman

period that "continues to command allegiances inconsistent with the full development of a modern

---

[72] McDowell, *A Modern History of the Kurds*, 3rd ed., 187.
[73] Van Bruissen, *Agah, Shaikh and State*, 13.
[74] "The PKK and Ethnic Terrorism in Turkey," *Ankara Papers,* 9 no. 1, (January 2004), 6.

nationalism."[75] The Sultans, though happy to have the Kurds as a military buffer, also worked to discourage greater Kurdish unions to dissuade a challenge to their own power.

Kurdish nomadic tribes first came under Ottoman control in 1516 with the Ottoman defeat of the Mamluks. This control was further consolidated with their subsequent defeat of the Savavids and capture of Baghdad in 1533.[76] This control was often tenuous as the physical separation between the capitol and Kurdish lands prevented direct supervision.[77] The isolation and remoteness of the region made greater control costly as Janissaries could not be tied up indefinitely subduing the eastern provinces while their services were required elsewhere in the Empire. The local Kurdish tribal leaders (*agahs*) were appointed as emirs by the Sultan to administer these territories much like the Sanjak Beys in other provinces.[78] This autonomy allowed a Kurdish identity to grow and conferred imperial recognition of the Kurdish tribal structure and leadership. Until the *Tanzimat* period, the Kurds were a substantial, independent political force. The *Tanzimat*, and its efforts to impose central control over the provinces, sought to undo this relationship.

The Empires' emirate system was able to hold the Kurdish tribes together in a loose union. The emirs themselves were tribal chiefs allocated sufficient lands, wealth, and arms to command the allegiance of neighboring tribes and their respective *agahs*.[79] Appointment of multiple emirs, covering different portions of the Kurdish regions, allowed the Sultans to maintain loyalty to themselves while simultaneously keeping power diffused among several entities. The *Tanzimat* reforms eliminated the emir system and, in so doing, had two profound effects. First, it fragmented control to the separate tribal *agahs* and secondly, strengthened the institution of *agah* and raised the prominence of another respected figure in the Kurdish culture, the *sheikh*.[80]

---

[75] Michael M. Gunter, *The Kurds in Turkey: A Political Dilemma* (Boulder: Westview Press, 1990), 5-6.

[76] McCarthey, *The Ottoman Turks*, 83.

[77] Van Bruissen, *Agah, Shaikh and State*, 135.

[78] Robert Olson, *The Emergence of Kurdish Nationalism and the Sheik Said Rebellion, 1880-1925* (Austin: University of Texas Press, 1989), xvi.

[79] Van Bruissen, *Agah, Shaikh and State*, 69.

[80] Ibid., 77.

The *sheikhs* represented an institution that cut across tribal divisions. *Sheikhs* were religious leaders that created personal followings based around their religious interpretations. *Sheikhs* commissioned deputies and created what Kurdish scholar Martin Van Bruissen termed "mafia-like" patronage systems based on personal loyalties and tithing.[81] The spiritual guidance and personal piety of the *sheikhs* made them traditional and trusted arbiters in tribal disputes. Their wealth also conferred a degree of worldly power. As *Tanzimat* stripped away the unity of the emirs, *sheikhs* and *agahs* were prepared to fill the void.

Historian Robert Olson identified four significant events that transpired from the *Tanzimat* period through the early republican period that fundamentally effected the development of Kurdish society. These stages were: (1) the Skeik Ubaydallah movement of the 1870s, (2) the formation of Hamidiya Cavalry Regiments, (3) the First World War and the Treaty of Sevres and (4) the rebellion of Sheik Said in 1925.[82] Abolition of the Kurdish emirates in favor of direct rule prompted a competition for local power among the various Kurd tribal leaders. Sheik Ubaydallah attempted to counter what he perceived as destructive infighting with a call for unity in the Islamic faith among the Kurdish tribes. The 1878 Treaty of Berlin, that ended the Russo-Turkish War, conceded a large portion of Ottoman territory to create an Armenian buffer state between Russia and Turkey. This prompted Sheikh Ubaydallah to act. Fearful that Kurdish tribal infighting and the presence of a non-Muslim entity to the east, the Ubaydallah organized a military expedition to organize the Kurds and remove the Armenian threat. His initial campaign, designed to lure Persian Kurds into a greater coalition, was militarily crushed by the Persians.[83] Though the movement garnered limited appeal and was defeated, it marked the beginning of a new relationship between the Ottomans and the Kurds.

Sultan Abdulhamid allowed the Persians to resolve the Sheikh Ubaydallah revolt, but the Treaty of Berlin and Ubeydallah's actions also forced him to reconsider the security situation in the

---

[81] Van Bruissen, *Agah, Shaikh and State*, 210.
[82] Olson, *The Emergence of Kurdish Nationalism and the Sheik Said Rebellion, 1880-1925*, 4.
[83] Ibid, 1.

east. Armenia and Russia posed a threat to the Empire. His means of addressing this threat focused on leveraging the Kurdish tribal structure to his advantage. In 1880, he authorized the formation of cavalry regiments recruited and led according to Kurdish tribal structures. The regiments were named in his honor as the Hamidaye Regiments. By 1895, 57 regiments were formed and were comprised of 65,000 Kurds. The military training as well as access to the same European education offered to the officers of the regular Ottoman Army, greatly enhanced not only Kurdish military organization along modern lines but also helped its greater political coherence to develop. Taken at face value, formation of such organizations appeared as extensions of the old emirates. The key distinction was that a large number of Kurds were now formally enrolled in the Imperial armies, and its leaders were availed to the same professional education as their non-Kurd contemporaries. This provided an organizational and intellectual base Kurd leaders were to leverage later on.[84]

The First World War provided the Kurds an opportunity to use this organization and education. Its true significance was realized only after the war's conclusion. Leading up to the First World War, Kurdish nationalism rode the coat tails of Young Turk nationalism. Kurdish nationalists were exposed to Western ideas much as the Ottoman officer corps was, and returned to the Kurdish region with very liberal ideas of nationalism. After the devastation of the war, where many of the Hamidiye Regiments and Kurdish conscripts fought and perished, the Treaty of Sevres offered an opportunity for the formalization of Kurdish nationalism. Acting on the promise of President Woodrow Wilson's Fourteen Points and the concept of self-determination, the Kurds were to be allotted an independent homeland in eastern Anatolia. In the late summer of 1920, impatient with the progress of Allied promises of autonomy, Kurd supporters of the nationalist ideal began forming in the Dersim region and, in October, began an open, armed revolt to create an autonomous Kurdistan. Lack of any outside support, divisions along tribal lines and confusion as to what the true aim of the

---

[84] Olson, *The Emergence of Kurdish Nationalism and the Sheik Said Rebellion, 1880-1925*, 7.

revolt doomed it to failure.[85] While the Dersim revolt failed, other forces were moving to terminate the promises of Versailles and Sevres. Ataturk was leading his revolution to establish the new Republic.

The Sheik Said rebellion marked the fourth major milestone in development of a Kurd nationalist identity. Sheik Said was 65 years old at the time of the rebellion and was a well known and respected religious leader in the Kurdish community. Galvanized by Ataturk's termination of the Caliphate, Sheik Said was determined to restore Islam as a fundamental pillar of the state and issued a *fatwa* in January 1925 condemning the Ankara government for destroying religion and stated it was lawful to rebel against it.[86] Armed hostilities against the Kemalists began on February 25, 1925 and, by April 15 of that same year, the revolt was crushed. Unable to persuade Kurdish Alevi tribes, who were primarily Shia and fearful of Kurdish Sunni domination, to join the revolt, the Kemalist forces were able to contain the fighting and defeat the Kurds in detail. Ataturk used this rebellion to introduce what David McDowell describes as "'implacable Kemalism'…systematic deportation and razing of villages, brutality and killing of innocents, martial law or special regimes in Kurdistan now became the commonplace experience of Kurds whenever they defied the state."[87] Suppression of the Kurds provided Ataturk with an opportunity to send a clear message to other would be separatists. "Implacable Kemalism" and its associated techniques were able to contain Kurdish nationalism for the next 50 years.

Robert Olson chronological evolution of the rise of Kurdish nationalism highlighted three important Kurdish characteristics as to how they relate to the Turkish state. The first was testifying to the existence of complex organizational structures and institutions that existed in the Kurdish culture. These traditional structures formed along tribal and religious identities wielded real power and influence over Kurdish society. Secondly, Olson illuminated that Islam had important social and

---

[85] Olson, *The Emergence of Kurdish Nationalism and the Sheik Said Rebellion, 1880-1925*, 33.
[86] Ibid., 94.
[87] McDowell, *A Modern History of the Kurds*, 3rd ed., 198.

political meaning to the Kurds to such a degree that sheikhs, traditionally pious men, could compel them to go to war. Finally, though tribes were important, the overall tribal structure was fragmented and susceptible to shifting loyalties. In evaluating the Turkish response to this Kurdish nationalism, particular patterns also emerge.

The first critical feature was the uncompromising attitude towards eradicating the Kurdish nationalist movement as a threat. Kurdish expert David McDowell wrote, "Turkey's attitude to its frontiers is special. It has an emotional and ideological view that its frontiers…cannot be changed without threatening the foundations of the Republic…the loss of Kurdistan…would be perceived as a grievous blow to the special identity of Turkey."[88] In order to maintain unity the Turks exploited the internal divisions along tribal lines to play loyalties against one another. They offered incentives to keep amenable tribes in the Turkish camp or helped to form alliances among friendly tribes in a policy of "divide and conquer". These policies were sufficient to keep Kurdish nationalism in check from the Sheik Said Rebellion through the 1970s. Changing political and economic conditions both domestically and internationally would alter the effectiveness of this approach.

---

[88] McDowell, *A Modern History of the Kurds*, 3rd ed., 7.

CHAPTER FIVE

Insurgency Theory

After nearly sixty years of relative calm, Kurdish nationalism re-emerged and turned violent
in the 1970s. Riding a wave of general, popular discontent among the Turkish polity, Kurdish groups
emerged to voice their displeasure about the poor economic conditions in the southeast. The coup of
1971 only temporarily suppressed the discontent, and by the middle of the decade, worsening
economic conditions and radicalization of the political process created volatile conditions. An
insurgency was allowed to take root because the undeniable conditions existed for its creation.
Historian Samuel Griffith wrote, "a potential revolutionary situation exists in any country where the
government consistently fails in its obligation to ensure at least a minimally decent standard of life for
the great majority of its citizens."[89] Perceived deprivation, whether for physical or psychological
needs, fuels an insurgency usually by providing its overall political goal. The Kurdish Worker's
Party (PKK) emerged from the eastern provinces as the voice of the Kurdish discontent.

The PKK declared its intention as the creation of a Kurdish state that would embody
socialist ideals.[90] They also declared its strategy would be based on the Maoist principles of
Revolutionary Warfare.[91] The PKK established a clear political goal and advocated a historically
effective method of achieving it. Mao Tse-tung suggested that guerrilla war is only part of the overall
political struggle. His two requirements for the struggle are "a clearly defined political goal" and that
it "must coincide with the aspirations of the people".[92] David Galula added that in addition to an
"attractive cause", insurgents require favorable geographic conditions and outside support in order to
be successful.[93] Based on these criteria, the Kurdish situation appeared promising for a successful

---

[89] Samuel B. Griffith, ed. and trans., *On Guerrilla Warfare*, by Mao Tse-tung (Urbana and Chicago: University of Illinois Press, 2000), 5-6.
[90] Gunter, *The Kurds in Turkey: A Political Dilemma*, 5-6.
[91] McDowell, *A Modern History of the Kurds*, 3rd ed., 422.
[92] Mao Tse-tung, *On Guerrilla War*, ed. and trans. Samuel B. Griffith (Urbana and Chicago: University of Illinois Press, 2000), 40-43.
[93] Galula, *Counter-Insurgency Warfare: Theory and Practice*, 21-40.

insurgency. Turkish repression, an emerging ethnic self-realization, mountainous terrain favorable for insurgency, and direct support garnered from external regional actors were facts that helped fulfill the requirements. Though conditions were favorable, the PKK was not able to capitalize on them. Though the struggle is not over, its conduct to date is a tale of missed opportunities and poor execution.

The PKK's insurgency has failed and been prolonged for four reasons. Principally, the PKK failed to reconcile its socialist message with the true strength of the Kurdish cause; namely, the unity provided by ethnic, Kurdish nationalism. By not aligning policies with the aspirations of the people, a fundamental pillar of Maoist revolution was missing. The PKK's next error was in not harmonizing its actions to its message. The PKK often treated Kurdish villagers as brutally as it did Turkish security forces. Their over reliance on violence, military campaigns, and terrorist attacks undermined any political or diplomatic programs it undertook. Not adequately addressing the cultural aspects of the struggle provided a third shortcoming. The PKK assaulted Turkish notions of nationalism directly, a key component of the Turkish state's strength, and did not leverage any asymmetrical advantage it may have had by attacking the state's stand on Westernization and Islam. The final point that acted to prolong the conflict was one not of the PKK's commission, but a sin of omission by the Turkish state. The uncompromising military campaign as the sole means of attacking the PKK left the Kurdish populous with few options. The PKK may not have been the perfect representation of Kurdish desires, but it offered the only alternative to economic deprivation and Turkish repression.

PKK Insurgency

Despite its Maoist pretensions, the PKK insurgency defies a standard definition as it does not fit comfortably into any existing model. Professing a Maoist strategy with socialist aims, it has frequently contorted its message and objectives as a matter of expediency. Socialism, nationalism, autonomy, and independence were all terms commonly referred to as goals by the PKK. Mao's contextual warning that his precepts of guerrilla warfare applied only to a revolutionary war, in

China, in the 1930s cannot explain away the PKK's indeterminacy. Failure of PKK leadership to latch on to a central political aim and employment of tactics commensurate with that strategic objective has proven to be a severe handicap.

Apo Ocalan and a small group of his associates formed the PKK in 1974. Marxism, not Kurdish nationalism, was at the heart of its formation. Its subsequently defined aim of Kurdish separatism, later downgraded to autonomy was seen as a means to spread socialist ideals, not carve out a Kurdish state.[94] Though not true nationalists, the organization sought that label for a number of reasons. A nationalist label acted as a public relations advantage since "by virtue of its being considered a nationalist organization the PKK seems to have inoculated itself against at least some of the damage that might be expected to result from reports of its murders, insurgent attacks and collaboration with a dictator [Syrian President Assad]."[95] Capitalization on the ethnic discontent in the Kurdish region was simply a convenient means to an end. The cloak of nationalism had its advantages in respect to the international audience, but produced clear liabilities in regards to its natural base of power, the Kurdish people in Turkey.

In regards to this natural support base, the strategic ambiguity produced two detrimental byproducts. First, by claiming the movement was the true aspiration of ethnic Kurds, it directly attacked Turkey's historic sense of hyper-nationalism. Kemalism could not tolerate a challenge to its concept of Turkishness.[96] While this nationalist call antagonized the Turks, its failure to reflect the identity of its target population, and employment of tactics which alienated this audience, undermined the PKK's effectiveness. Political scientist Michael Radu cited three main reasons for the PKKs lack of representation or close affiliation with the Turkish Kurds. First, ethnic Turks and non-Kurds have long been a part of the organization as Ocalan recruited heavily from neighboring sources, particularly Syria. Secondly, Ocalan himself is not ethnically Kurd; he was of Turkoman origin.

---

[94] Michael Radu, "The Rise and Fall of the PKK," *Orbis* 45, no. 2 (Winter 2001): 5.
[95] Ibid., 5.
[96] McDowell, *A Modern History of the Kurds*, 3rd ed., 7.

Finally, the organization alienated neighboring Kurds due to its frequent alliances of convenience with the oppressive regimes of Syria, Iran and Iraq; all of which savagely repressed or discriminated against their own ethnic Kurds.[97] In the early stages of its military campaign, PKK fighters targeted Kurdish villages suspected of Turk sympathies and were insensitive to the further deprivations of townspeople caused by their war. Usually safe in its sanctuaries in Syria and Iraq, these discomforts of the people were not shared by the PKK.

Despite the problem of not adequately reflecting its popular base, the PKK was allowed to flourish due to the presence of neighbors friendly to their efforts. As political conditions worsened within Turkey, the PKK moved its base of operations into Syrian territory just prior to the Turkish military coup in 1981. Establishing a base of operations within Syria, with that government's tacit consent, the PKK was able to build its organization without interference. In its second congress held in 1982, the PKK formulated a Marxist strategy "of three broad phases: defense, balance and offense."[98] In the strategic defense it planned to wage armed propaganda and recruit before entering the next phase in 1995. The balance phase was aimed at creating liberated zones where it could marshal forces and organize the populous for the final, decisive phase. They did not anticipate that this phase would commence until after the year 2000.[99] With the protection of Syria, the PKK made great progress in its efforts to organize throughout the 1980s. It established the Kurdistan Popular Liberation Front (ERNK) as its political wing in 1985 to complement its Kurdistan Peoples' Liberation Army (ARGK) which acted as its guerrilla army. The ERNK focused on urban organization, propaganda, and recruitment while the ARGK was a rurally based, military entity. By 1996, the ARGK reached its peek fighting strength of 35,000 with an equally robust urban support network of the ERNK.[100]

---

[97] Radu, "The Rise and Fall of the PKK," 3.
[98] McDowell, *A Modern History of the Kurds*, 3rd ed., 422.
[99] Gunter, *The Kurds and the Future of Turkey*, 47.
[100] Ibid., 38.

Protected in the Syrian provided sanctuary, the PKK was able to prosecute its military centered campaign. The PKK set its initial goal as eliminating its political competition and breaking the traditional structures of power in the southeast region.[101] These structures included large landowners, absentee landlords and the strong tribal system. By the late 1970s and early 1980s, the traditional feudal lands evolved into a system no less restrictive than the *agah* dominated system of the Ottoman Empire. Large plots of land were farmed on behalf of wealthy landowners residing in the west while its tenants struggled to survive on plots granted to them for subsistence. Little to no wealth produced through agriculture was retained in the Kurdish areas. PKK actions against the *agahs* were appreciated by the unempowered Kurds. Dealing with the tribal system proved more troublesome. Playing on tribal animosities, the PKK was able to garner assistance, but it also acquired new enemies. Initially the populous demonstrated very little sympathy for PKK activities since Kurds were the primary targets of violence. This attitude changed when Turk security forces became the target of their violence in the early to mid 1980s. This enthusiasm flagged again; however when Turkish forces began targeting PKK collaborators. The PKK then followed suit by attacking Kurd villages found supporting government operations as a means to dissuade other villages from doing the same. In a repeating cycle of violence, recrimination and escalation, the Kurdish citizenry bore the brunt of the pain while seeing very little benefit.[102] Realizing the negative impact these policies were having, the PKK made the decision to transition to mobile warfare in 1988 ahead of their intended schedule and limit their military activity to Turkish Army targets only. Such a strategy looked very promising, but the move to offensive war proved premature.

The PKK was able to conduct active and sustained operations due to the transnational support it received in territory, funding and other support, and in its ability to maintain a level of appeal both within and outside of Turkey. The PKK was clearly used as a proxy by both Syria and Iran to cause

---

[101] Umit Ozdag and Ersel Aydinli, "Winning Low Intensity Conflict: Drawing Lessons from the Turkish Case," *Review of International Affairs* 2, no. 3 (Spring 2003), 106.
[102] Ibid.,108.

problems for its regional competitor, the state of Turkey. Both states provided sanctuary, funding, and in the case of Syria, intelligence support to the PKK. The Soviet Union indirectly supported Syria's efforts in an effort to destabilize this key member of NATO.[103] On its own account, the PKK proved adept at maintaining a sophisticated financial operation. Relying on the Kurdish expatriate community in Europe and investments in various enterprises, some legal but mostly in drug-trafficking, the PKK was able to draw in nearly US$100 million per year.[104] This external support and secure sanctuary allowed the PKK to offset the deficiencies of poor identification with its base and reliance on a military solution, but it could not compensate for some missed opportunities.

Moving so rapidly to mobile warfare may have blinded the PKK to a tremendous opportunity. The PKK did not appeal to Islam or the natural distrust of Westernization as a means to manipulate the tensions of the Turkish Construct. The local Islamic practices were important to Kurdish culture.[105] The PKK leadership acknowledged this as early as 1988, but failed to act on it. Its politburo declared in an internal document that "in the realities of the Middle East, there is no way of leading a successful revolution without taking account of the importance of the people's religion. Ignorance of religion causes a counter-revolution which inevitably prepares our defeat."[106] The PKK's appeal to religion never became more than a façade. The socialist message continued to predominate. Many of the nation's Muslims, though members of a republic, still respect the idea of the umma, the popular concept of a greater Islamic community. Continued repression of a Muslim community offered the potential of gathering support from sympathetic non-Kurd Muslims.[107] The PKK also failed to appeal to another common Kurdish trait, poverty.

---

[103] Umit Ozdag and Ersel Aydinli, "Winning Low Intensity Conflict: Drawing Lessons from the Turkish Case," 107.

[104] Gunter, *The Kurds and the Future of Turkey*, 57.

[105] Dodd, *Democracy and Development in Turkey*, 48.

[106] "The PKK and Ethnic Terrorism in Turkey," 31.

[107] Tapper, ed. *Islam in Modern Turkey*, 4.

A survey conducted by the Turkish Chamber of Commerce (TOBB) in August 1995 offered a

glimpse at what truly mattered to Kurdish citizens.[108] A newspaper summarized the report's findings

with the following analogy: "the PKK can be compared to a train. The militant nucleus of the

organization aims at arriving at the station of complete independence. However, the local people are

ready to step out…when they arrive at the stops of more independence in regard to their daily lives,

income, job, education, health, respect for identity…and cultural lives."[109] The report itself

concluded, "the solution does not lie with the PKK. An agreement should be reached with the people

of the area."[110] A campaign that appealed more to social injustice, material deprivation and identity

would have had greater appeal.

The net result of these omissions was the PKKs inability to appeal and ultimately control the

population. In an insurgency, the side that controls the population will win the war. Only a campaign

that uses military action to further a political goal and win over the populous can succeed. Galula

argued that political action "remains the foremost instrument and every military move has to be

weighed with regard to its political effects."[111] The PKK never seriously made an effort to win the

population to their cause. Galula also wrote, "The complicity of the population is not to be confused

with the sympathy of the population; the former is active and the latter inactive, and the popularity of

the insurgent's cause is insufficient in itself to transform sympathy into complicity. The participation

…is obtained by a political organization living among the population backed by force."[112] The PKK

was not able to establish a political objective in tune with the population's desires nor reconcile their

political objective with its use of force. Ocalan never achieved a unity of effort. This violated Mao's

conception that "guerrilla war largely depends upon powerful political leaders who work unceasingly

to bring about internal unification. Such leaders must work with the people; they must have a correct

---

[108] Gunter, *The Kurds and the Future of Turkey*, 127.
[109] Sinan Yilmaz, "Chamber of Commerce Report on Kurds Detailed," *Ankara Turkish Daily News*, 4 August 1995, A2.
[110] Ibid., A2.
[111] Galula, *Counter-Insurgency Warfare: Theory and Practice*, 7-8.
[112] Ibid., 50.

conception of the policy to be adopted in regards to both the people and the enemy."[113] The PKK did

not develop or execute an effective insurgency plan, but to the PKK's advantage, the Turkish

government's response was also less than adequate.

[113] Tse-tung, *On Guerrilla War*, 63.

CHAPTER SIX

Counter-Insurgency Theory and the Turkish Campaign

The principle objective of a state in conducting a counter-insurgency campaign is a restoration of control over its entire territory. This tangible objective is paralleled by a moral one of resolving the underlying conflict to establish a lasting peace. Essentially, the counter-insurgency force must remove the insurgent's reason for being. Counter-insurgency theorist David Galula wrote "that to deprive the insurgent of a good cause amounts to solving the country's basic problems. If this is possible, well and good, but we know now that a good cause for the insurgent is one that his opponent cannot adopt without losing his power in the process and there are problems that, although providing a good cause to the insurgent, are not susceptible of solution."[114] The state is then left with three broad sets of options. It may concede to the insurgent's demands, deny the insurgents any latitude and undermine their position completely, or seek to meet the insurgency movement with some form of compromise. The Turkish state decided upon the second course, which in itself is not a poor selection. Turkish policy towards the PKK presented two options to the enemy: be killed or be captured. This narrow approach; however, was problematic as it violated the basic tenets of counter-insurgency. Galula referred to them as his five laws of counter-insurgency.

Galula proposed five laws to guide the conduct of counter-insurgencies. The first law of counter-insurgency was that support of the population was vital to both the insurgent and the counter-insurgent. Second, this support must be sustained by the active support of a minority and each side must win over, and rally the neutral elements of society to their camp. The third law was the understanding that support of the population, even of the initial minority, was conditional and must be continually cultivated. Fourth, in order to achieve a lasting effect on the population, there must be an intensity of effort and a vastness of means to keep the population tied to one camp. Finally, victory

---

[114] Galula, *Counter-Insurgency Warfare: Theory and Practice*, 67.

was achieved through the permanent isolation of the insurgent from the population with active help from the population itself.[115] Both sides of the conflict had a common, overriding objective; namely, the control of the population, and must adhere to similar considerations in its efforts towards this end. There were also essential differences that characterize the methods that can be employed by each camp.

The most obvious of these was that the insurgent had the initiative. Rare circumstances would have to exist where a state would be able to take pre-emptive action to stop a violent insurgency from emerging. The physical aspects of counter-insurgency would have to remain idle until "the insurgent has clearly revealed his intentions by engaging in subversion or open violence, he represents nothing but an imprecise, potential menace to the counter-insurgent and does not offer a concrete target that would justify a large effort."[116] Transition from discontent and political action to open warfare occurred at the initiation by the insurgent. The second fundamental difference involves the levels of restraint imposed on the counter-insurgency force, or lack of these restraints on the insurgent. Maintaining order was the imperative function of the state and this was an expensive proposition. It is much less expensive for the insurgent to cause chaos and disorder. Regular forces were at a disadvantage as they are reliant on their lines of supply while an insurgent was free of such restrictions. Freedom from constraints dealt also with the methodology employed. Every insurgency was different and its perpetrators were free to improvise and use different methods.[117] Much like the case of the initiative, the counter-insurgent must take the time to study the methods of his enemies and adapt his strategies and tactics to meet the current needs. Once the enemy was understood, the time is right for the development and implementation of the plan.

Three problems with the Turkish approach emerged when compared to the theoretical underpinnings of counter-insurgency. These were the state's resolution to approach the problem from

---

[115] Galula, *Counter-Insurgency Warfare: Theory and Practice*, 74-77.
[116] Ibid., 3.
[117] C. E. Caldwell, *Small Wars: Their Principles and Practice* (Lincoln: University of Nebraska Press, 1996), 33.

a single perspective, its proclivity to address the symptoms of the underlying problem and not the central problem itself and misinterpreting the origins of the conflict. The Turkish military consistently beat the PKK in the field but the insurgents kept regenerating and created a near constant state of instability. Similarly, a force on force solution failed to undermine the general sources of discontent in the Kurdish region. Poverty, unemployment, and cultural discrimination persisted. Perhaps the most egregious of errors was casting the conflict in terms acceptable to the Kemalist vision. The Turks did not understand their enemy as what it was, but what they wished it to be. The good cause of the insurgent, Kurdish ethnicity and perceived relative deprivation, were not vulnerable to the force of arms. Turks perceive the PKK as terrorists and the Kurds as misguided Turks. As a consequence, the population was something to be cowed and not won over. The Turks preferred the military option, but they have tried to incorporate other elements of national power into their overall campaign. Attempts at leveraging diplomatic, informational, and economic components coupled with the military element have come up short in large part to their persistent cultural bias. A review of the actions taken across the elements of national power helps provide a clearer understanding of this bias.

The Turkish Campaign – Diplomatic

The Ottoman legacy, Kemalist perceptions of nationalism and Islam were the three most influential factors in fashioning the Turks diplomatic and political response to the PKK. Ataturk and his fellow nationalists believed the Ottoman reliance on tolerance of minorities for the sake of nominal unity only weakened the empire.[118] The Ottoman's recipe for union was Islam. This, and the Quran's intrinsic protection for people of the book (*dhimmi*), relied on tolerance as the lubricant for the easement of ethnic tension. Alternatively, the Ataturk Republic accentuated conformity to a central identity over any notions of tolerance.[119] The 1923 Treaty of Lausanne maintained trappings of Ottoman tolerance by recognizing the protected minorities as Greeks, Armenians and Jews, but it

---

[118] Zulkuf Aydin, "Uncompromising Nationalism: The Kurdish Question in Turkey," in *The Politics of Permanent Crisis*, ed. Nesecan Balkan and Sungur Savran (New York: Nova Science, 2002), 87.
   [119] Ibid., 87.

did not yield any provision of autonomy to these groups. These minority protections were insisted upon by the Western powers still leery of Muslim intentions and practices. This left the Kurds, close to autonomy in the Treaty of Sevres as an obvious source of conflict. The magnitude of the threat was quickly realized with the Sheik Said rebellion. Ataturk dealt three blows to the Kurds that helped precipitate a Kurdish response: these were the negation of thee Treaty of Sevres, supplanting the Sultan and eliminating the Caliphate. Ataturk's subsequent legislative actions clearly identified the Kurds as a people to be converted. Law 2510, issued in this period, divided Turkey into three zones, areas representative of Turkish culture, regions requiring indoctrination and regions requiring complete evacuation. All southeast territories were in the later category. Additionally, Law 1850 ensured "no one engaged in suppressing the Kurds could be prosecuted for any excess."[120] These laws prompted some relocations as well as the use of *ocaks* which were indoctrination committees sent out into "Kurdistan to persuade the population to be good Turks."[121] Relocation and re-education efforts were sufficient only to suppress the problem and not address the underlying tensions.

Coercion and conversion were at the heart of the government's attitude and the armed forces were the agents and main proponents of this approach. The political and military instruments of government cannot be considered in isolation from one another. Post Ataturk political activities were conducted in the shadow of a praetorian military. Military influence on the Republic restricted the range of political options available to policy makers. The military occupied "the paradoxical position of safeguarding democracy while at the same time posing a major challenge to further democratization."[122] The military is both an enabler of the military campaign yet an obstruction to the pursuit of practical political engagement to resolve the underlying social problems. In protecting

---

[120] McDowell, *A Modern History of the Kurds*, 3rd ed., 206.

[121] Ibid., 201.

[122] Binnaz Toprak, "Islam and Democracy in Turkey," *Turkish Studies*, 6 no. 2, (June 2005), 179.

the Republic and exercising its rights in the Kemalist model as the Republic's ultimate guardian, the military hindered the prosecution of the counter-insurgency.

Militarily inspired political action to deal with the PKK centered on coercion and control and the imposition of martial and emergency laws were the instruments of this policy. From 1961 to the last direct intervention coup in 1980, civil liberties were increasingly restricted. The strength and latitude granted to the MGK grew on pace, eventually acquiring the right to give binding advice to the Cabinet. Its reaction to the activities of the Refah government in 1996 was indicative of its influence and willingness to use it. The series of Emergency Laws passed between 1984 and 2002 created a "super-governor" responsible for the seven main provinces of discontent: Diyarbakir, Elazig, Siirt, Sirnak, Tuncelli, Van, and Batman.[123] The location of these provinces may be found in the appendix. The super-governor, a lieutenant general in the Turkish Armed Forces, was granted broad powers to command all security forces to include police, given authority to conduct intrusive searches, and control all civilian movement.[124] The governor was also allowed to relocate entire villages if residents were "known or likely to disturb public order."[125] By 1998, nearly 1000 villages and 300,000 people were relocated.[126] Local military commanders of the region also had broad powers to ban public strikes or demonstrations, suspend the media and dismiss local officials.[127] Such policies proved effective in disrupting PKK activities, but also severely restricted the liberties of local inhabitants and exacerbated the economic deprivation of the region.

The connection between the relative deprivation of the region and the PKK insurgency was frequently considered, but seldom acted on. Since 1990, several proposals surfaced to resolve the Kurdish issue. In March 1993, then Prime Minister Turgut Ozal "was convinced that peace could be

---

[123] Amikam Nachmani, *Turkey: Facing a New Millennium* (Manchester and New York: Manchester University Press, 2003), 47.

[124] Republic of Turkey. 1993. *State of Emergency Law Act 2935*. Chapter 3, Article 1, para. (a)-(p). 25 October 1993; available from http://www.law.qub.ac.uk/humanrts/emergency/turkey/tur4.htm.

[125] Republic of Turkey. 1990. *Decree 430*. Article 1 para. (b)-(c). 16 December 1990: available from http://www.law.qub.ac.uk/humanrts/emergency/turkey/tur7.htm.

[126] Global Internally Displaced Person Database. "State of Emergency in Southeastern Turkey: Severe Restriction of Human Rights," available from *http://www.db.idpproject.org*.

[127] Hale, *Turkish Politics and the Military*, 251.

achieved only through negotiations with the PKK and that a ceasefire was essential."[128] Ozal's sudden death a month later brought this initiative to a halt. Comprehensive rebuilding plans began surfacing again in 1996 when the Refah Party proposed an economic development plan.[129] In September of 2000, the Turkish press revealed a government report acknowledged the social dimension of the problem and that conditions were made worse through poor public administration, poor economic conditions and poor education.[130] Then Chief of the General Staff, General Huseyin Kivrikoglu commented on the topic in an interview in February 2002. He announced that the MGK issued a 107 article plan of action for the Southeast to the government. The general also claimed the military sent their "brightest" to the region while, "sadly there are problems in terms of the remaining public personnel."[131] As recently as August 2005, Prime Minister Edrogan, in a speech at Diyarbakir, confessed "mistakes have been made" in how the government handled the region. He also stated there were three "red lines" that could not be broached in solving the Kurdish question. These were: (1) ethnic nationalism, (2) regional nationalism, and (3) religious nationalism.[132] Despite the list of programs proposed, the political dialogue remained tightly conformed within Kemalist parameters. As a consequence, plans remained plans and were not translated into real action.

The Turkish Campaign – Informational

It was apparent that the Turkish government and security apparatus tried to shape the conflict into what they will it to be rather than accepting it as what it actually was. The Turkish government has attempted to "strip the Kurdish problem from its ethnic, cultural, and international contents and present it as a question of terrorism and misplaced developmental strategies."[133] A narrow vision of

---

[128] Robert Olson, ed., *The Kurdish National Movement in the 1990s* (Lexington: University Press of Kentucky, 1996), 15.

[129] Kemal Balci, "RP Plan for Southeast Reported," *Ankara Turkish Daily News*. 23 August 1996, 1.

[130] Fikret Bila, "Government Gears Up for Action in the Southeast," *Istanbul Milliyet*, 14 September 2000, 16.

[131] Yavuy Donat, "TSK and GAP," *Istanbul Sabah*. 19 February 2002, 1.

[132] "Prime Minister Edrogan in Diyarbakir", *Ankara Anatolian*, 12 August 2005, 1.

[133] Aydin, "Uncompromising Nationalism: The Kurdish Question in Turkey," 86.

the problem and unwillingness to accept alternative viewpoints has conditioned policies, strategy and responses to PKK violence. Colonel Yuksel Oztekin, a Turkish officer, wrote a monograph entitled "Terrorism in Turkey" at the US Army War College in 2000. His perspective and opinion on the conflict with the PKK was quite obviously displayed throughout the document and a review of these sentiments may provide a narrow, but likely representative, view of the Turkish officer corps.

The author stated that "there is no Kurdish problem in Turkey" and asserted that the Turkish government does not reject "the identity of the Kurdish people" and that the problem was with the PKK alone which is comprised of "lower class ghetto youths...self-styled Marxists".[134] Colonel Oztekin goes to great pains to illustrate the commonality of language and culture between the two groups. He concludes that the Kurds did not emerge in 1923 as a true national movement due to their "lack of ethnic self-awareness" and declared that "Turks and Kurds were brothers in terms of race and religion."[135] The author's logic becomes disjointed at times as he goes on to characterize "Kurdishness" as an identity of "tribal divisions and of a population scattered largely across what came to be the Persian and Ottoman empires...the fact that the Kurds are widely scattered throughout Turkey...attests to the dispersal of the Kurds."[136] Regardless if these assertions were based on fact or on socialized and indoctrinated official history, they represented the beliefs and attitudes of a significant part of the Turkish military establishment. This perception produced two key and inter-related features of the Turkish informational effort. These are a contradiction in messages and a failure to adequately explain the conflict to both its internal constituency and foreign audiences.

Zulkuf Aydin helps to identify the problems with the dual message. Citing Professor Cizre-Sakalliglu, he writes "Turkish nationalism has been based on 'two contradictory elements, an ethno-cultural dimension highlighting the ethnic singularity of Turkishness and a modern civil component which essentially grants equal citizenship rights to all those in Turkish territory'...the inclusion of

---

[134] Yuksel Oztekin, "Terrorism in Turkey" (Masters Thesis, US Army War College, 2000), vii.
[135] Ibid., 5.
[136] Ibid., 14.

such contradiction…is not the result of an innocent mistake but that of a deliberate intention of being able to have recourse to either of them if necessary."[137] The Turkish state perpetuated a confusing dichotomy of suppressing Kurdishness while accepting it as part and parcel of Turkishness. More simply stated, the Turks cannot deny the existence of Kurdishness while simultaneously pursuing a policy of ethnic conversion. Either Kurdishness existed and required conversion or it did not. This contorted logic was difficult to explain and defies comprehension by those outside the problem. Perhaps this difficult message was the reason the Turkish government has not tried to use the informational element to its advantage. The Turkish government has portrayed the problem as simple and one dimensional and failed to convey what real importance the issue has to the state. The state has not leveraged propaganda to the fullest extent.

The Turkish Campaign – Economic

Economic approaches have similarly floundered. Colonel Oztekin's reference to "lower class ghetto youths" was not entirely inaccurate. Much of the PKK's base comes from the poor and dispossessed. This is in large part due to the relative economic deprivation of the region and failure of the Turkish government to address the oppressive economic conditions. Economic data released in the early 1990s revealed that per capita income in the traditionally Kurdish regions of Turkey was 42% that of the national average.[138] The region suffered the ills of an agrarian society still based on feudal structures. Traditional land ownership in the hands of agahs and absentee landlords kept land plots small and thus kept those tilling the land at nearly subsistence level of farming.[139] The lack of adequate infrastructure only compounded the problem as the southeast was isolated from any capital flows due to its isolation. Efforts to remedy this disparity have been reluctant, incomplete and misplaced.

---

[137] Zulkuf Aydin, "Uncompromising Nationalism: The Kurdish Question in Turkey," 90.
[138] McDowell, *A Modern History of the Kurds*, 3rd ed., 447.
[139] Toprak, "Islam and Democracy in Turkey," 180.

Turkey faced an economic conundrum. It was too poor to develop the region alone yet its wealthy Western sponsors withheld funds to pressure a resolution on the Kurdish question.[140] Statism, one of the six components of Kemalism, was divined as a temporary fix by Ataturk to break the new Republic out of antiquated Ottoman economic practices.[141] Throughout the 1960s and 1970s, privatization and attempts to finance development through internal means proved insufficient. The Turkish government was forced to seek assistance from the International Monetary Fund (IMF) and World Bank whose proscription of "cutting wages, eliminating unnecessary jobs and devaluing the currency" hit the country hard.[142] Turgut Ozal was brought into the government by the MGK for his abilities as an economist in the 1980s and his austerity measures brought some relief but also wild fluctuations in the Turk economy. Turkish scholar Amikam Nachmani wrote "Turkey's economy is a strange combination of enormous success and huge failures. The country keeps swinging back and forth between prosperity and recession. Success, prosperity, inflation, stagnation, and recession were a peculiar mixture hardly explained by experts and academics."[143] Turkey's economic conditions certainly limited use of economics as an instrument to resolve the PKK insurgency.

Another characteristic of Turk economic programs was the military nature of its implementation.[144] A large part of the economic efforts are designed and led by the military.[145] Military units executed large construction projects, provided logistics, and conducted vocational training. This was largely a product of the prevailing security situation in the eastern provinces as the endemic violence kept civilian administrators away. The military also operated a series of economic enterprises which by 1990 employed 40,000 people.[146] The military's programs operated despite the lack of an overall, comprehensive plan. Desperation over this fact prompted the MGK to issue a

---

[140] Blank, Pelletier, and Johnson, *Turkey's Strategic Position at the Crossroads of World Affairs*, 97.

[141] Dodd, *Democracy and Development in Turkey*, 87.

[142] Blank, Pelletier, and Johnson, *Turkey's Strategic Position at the Crossroads of World Affairs*, 43.

[143] Nachmani, *Turkey: facing a New Millennium*, 75.

[144] Fikret Bila, "Investment in People," *Istanbul Millayet*, 14 October 2000, 16.

[145] Ersel Aydinli, "Between Security and Liberalization: Decoding Turkey's Struggle with the PKK," *Security Dialogue*, 33 no. 2 (June 2002), 218.

[146] Nachmani, *Turkey: Facing a New Millennium*, 95.

statement in 1999 that it would be the lead agency in the redevelopment of the southeast.[147]

Economic programs for the southeast have focused on a single project.

The Southeast Anatolia Project (GAP) was designed to produce a massive hydro-electrical system to bring prosperity to the region. Critics questioned the true impact of the project as "it was difficult to see how a largely illiterate population would be able to benefit from capital intensive agriculture or agro-industry, let alone the ancillary sector that would crop up to receive it. The Kurds had neither capital nor education."[148] GAP benefits would extend to the industrialized western regions that were already equipped to leap ahead with access to a new source of inexpensive energy. Completion of the GAP is still sometime off in the future. Interim measures by the Turkish government included a $102 million allocation to create 8,200 jobs in 1999. The same year $31 billion was allocated in an 8 year military modernization program.[149] This indicated where the true priorities laid.

The Turkish Campaign – Military

The military option has been the Turkish state's preferred solution to the PKK insurgency. The Turkish Construct has ultimately shaped the Turkish response in this direction. The struggles between nationalism, Westernization, and Islam created what Turkish political scientist Ersel Aydinli termed a "national security syndrome". Throughout the Ottoman-Turkish experience reformers have liberalized in order to protect the state, while simultaneously fearing liberalization and decentralization as dangerous. This syndrome was perpetuated because those responsible for security have also led the reforms.[150] Self-designated as the praetorian guard of Kemalism, the military found itself on four major occasions as the only entity capable of saving the Republic from itself.[151] The

---

[147] Nuri Sefa Erden, "Turkey's NSC to Discuss Changes in the Southeast," *Istanbul Yeni Yuzyil*, 19 February, 7.

[148] McDowell, *A Modern History of the Kurds*, 3rd ed. 447.

[149] Ibid., 448.

[150] Aydinli, "Between Security and Liberalization: Decoding Turkey's Struggle with the PKK," 210.

[151] Hale, *Turkish Politics and the Military*, 304.

Turkish military made it its business to protect the Republic and its territorial and political sovereignty at all costs. Contributing to these attitudes was the sense that the officer corps represented the enlightened elite and could act with greater independence from the rest of society by virtue of this enlightenment. Army officers acted as the vanguard of political reform in ending Ottoman Rule and forming the Republic and this sense of history has never departed. Turkish officers accepted that civil authorities should rule over the military, but that they reserved the right to intervene when the life of the state was in jeopardy. The threat of Kurdish separatism and the PKK in particular has always been portrayed as a direct threat to the survival of the Republic. Framing the problem in such a manner left the Turkish military, and therefore the Turkish state, with little intellectual discretion in addressing the problem.

The campaign against the PKK was characterized by three general phases. From 1979 to 1986, the Turkish Army fought the PKK as a counter-terrorism effort. After 1986 and the lifting of martial law and shift to the Emergency period, the military took a less active role in the Southeast provinces as pressures over Cyprus shifted their attention. Beginning in 1992, the military again asserted itself and organized a counter-insurgency fight.[152] Military success was attributed to two main reasons. First, the Turkish military's adoption of clear and hold tactics in 1995 allowed for a gradual pacification of territory and, secondly, cutting off the PKK's international sources of supply, funding and support.[153]

The clear and hold tactic was enabled by redirecting resources and adopting an old Ottoman practice.[154] Initially the problem of the PKK was "under-whelmed" with resources. The general instability of the late 1970s masked much of the PKK's organizational period and was therefore allowed to build strength then seek sanctuary within Syria. Insufficient forces, poor intelligence and insufficient infrastructure to accommodate a modern military initially plagued Turkish Army efforts

---

[152] Umit Ozdag and Ersel Aydinli, "Winning Low Intensity Conflict: Drawing Lessons from the Turkish Case," 103.

[153] Nachmani, *Turkey: facing a New Millennium*, 43-44.

[154] McCarthey, *The Ottoman Turks*, 124.

in the southeast regions.[155] Such obstacles prevented the Army from offering the most basic

protection to loyal villages. To make up for this deficiency, the Turkish military revitalized a

program called the "Village Guards". Initially adopted in the 1920s to play upon the local tribal

rivalries, tribes and villages were ordered or commissioned to create local security structures.

Reinstituted in April 1985, the Village Guards were drawn from traditionally loyal tribes then

expanded to include tribes with particular grievances against the PKK.[156] Recruits were paid an

average of $230 per month when the annual per capita income in the region was only $100.[157] When

inducement did not work, impressments backed up by retribution became the Turkish means of

recruitment into the system. The Village Guard system was designed in part to demonstrate the

traditional divisions of the Kurdish movement. Tribal loyalties did in fact trump ethnic identification

on many occasions and it was a fact the Turkish government again sought to accentuate.[158] The PKK

turned its attention on the Village Guards in 1987 with a ruthless campaign designed to eradicate

villages which sponsored such organizations. Such measures forced many supportive groups to

disassociate themselves from the PKK. Principally important among these was the KDP. PKK

counter reprisals on loyal PKK villages characterized an intensifying viciousness to the entire

struggle.

A state of emergency was declared for the Kurdish regions in 1987, and the following years

brought successively more repressive measures. After responding the Aegean crisis, Turkish military

organizations returned in full force beginning in 1991 and announced a "battlefield domination

concept" as their new strategy.[159] This particular strategy involved reorganizing conventional units

into internal security battalions, advocated brigade vice division based organizations as the basis for

---

[155]Umit Ozdag and Ersel Aydinli, "Winning Low Intensity Conflict: Drawing Lessons from the Turkish Case," 108.

[156] Global Internally Displaced Database, "State of Emergency in Southeastern Turkey: Severe Restrictions of Human Rights," available from *http://www.db.idpproject.org.*

[157] McDowell, *A Modern History of the Kurds*, 3rd ed., 425.

[158] Robbins, "The Overlord State: Turkish Policy and the Kurdish Issue," 664.

[159] Umit Ozdag and Ersel Aydinli, "Winning Low Intensity Conflict: Drawing Lessons from the Turkish Case," *Democracies and Small Wars*, 111.

counter-insurgency organization and committing to cross-border operations into Iraq. Such incursions were negotiated with Baghdad and even enlisted the support of the KDP and PUK. Since 1984, the Turkish Army crossed into Iraq no less than 57 times.[160] In 1993, the MGK, now in full control of policy in the Southeast, instituted a broad relocation program and maintained continuous military pressure on the PKK.[161] Turkish efforts also included unique adaptations. Principal among these was the use of a paramilitary organization affiliated with the National Action Party (NAP).[162] The 1981 coup and the resultant attitude that greater firmness was required to restore order empowered several conservative parties. Desiring to maintain loyalty in this base, the ruling party granted ultra-conservative parties like the NAP authority to integrate into the Village Guards as officers and create commando groups to pursue the PKK.[163]

The military campaign culminated in October 1998 when Turkey massed 10,000 troops on the Syrian border and demanded that Ocalan be turned over. This military push coincided with an overt outreach towards Israel to force Syria between two potentially hostile powers. The Turkish ultimatum and international pressure compelled Ocalan's departure. In a circuitous journey that saw Ocalan visit Russia, Italy, and Greece; Ocalan ultimately arrived in Kenya in hopes of finding asylum. On February 1, 1999, with assistance from US intelligence and Kenyan participation, Turkish security agents apprehended Ocalan in Kenya.

The Turkish Campaign – Assessment

Turkish scholar Ersil Aydinli noted in 2002 that "Turkey has emerged from a 15 year struggle against the Kurdish PKK movement with a decisive military victory…nevertheless, there are strong indicators that a new political struggle between Turkey and the PKK…has only just begun."[164]

---

[160] Jung and Piccoli, *Turkey at the Crossroads*, 145.
[161] McDowell, *A Modern History of the Kurds*, 3rd ed., 440.
[162] Jung and Piccoli, *Turkey at the Crossroads*, 118.
[163] Tim Jacoby, "For the People, Of the People, and by the Military: The Regime Structure of Modern Turkey," *Political Studies* 51 (2003), 676.
[164] Aydinli, "Between Security and Liberalization: Decoding Turkey's Struggle with the PKK," 209.

Aydinli's comments were a response to the recent PKK name change to Kongra-Gel and formation of its new militant wing, the People's Defense Forces (HPG).[165] Consequently, armed resistance resumed in 2003 with a parallel political effort with the newly formed Freedom and Democracy Congress of Kurdistan (KADEK), the new political wing of the Kongra-Gel/PKK.[166] It appeared that, despite Ocalan's arrest, the struggle would continue in a new form.

In a report by the *New Anatolian* newspaper on January 7, 2006, the military high command issued three messages to the government. Alarmed by Prime Minister Erbakan's speech at Diyarbakir and the apparent softening in policies with reference to the PKK, the military issued three warnings. The newspaper reported that the messages were: (1) the military fights terrorists but the government as a whole needs to fight terrorism, (2) terrorists should not be allowed to gain political legitimacy, and (3) recent government practices that encouraged religious education should be curtailed. The military also complained about new regulations that required local military commanders to seek approval from the local governor before conducting counter-terrorism operations.[167] Kemalism, and the role of the military, remained a critical component to how the new threat was to be addressed and therefore a roadblock to any dialogue on the Kurdish issue.

---

[165] Terrorism Knowledge Database, "HPG," available from http://www.tKb.org.

[166] "A Roadmap from KADEK," *Neu-Isenburg Ozgur Politika*, 12 August 2003.

[167] Evren Deger, "Three Messages From the Military of Terror," *Ankara The New Anatolian*, 7 January 2006, 1.

CHAPTER SEVEN

Lessons – Theory and Practice of Insurgent Wars

David Galula offered a step by step process for the conduct of counter-insurgency campaigns. Galula's process essentially involved the removal of the insurgent military and political structures, consolidating these gains and installing the new elements of civilian control. C.E. Caldwell, renowned theorist and practitioner of counter-insurgency warfare, offered other supporting considerations of Galula's themes. Caldwell emphasizes the methodical and progressive clearing of sectors and warns drawing the enemy out will be the counter-insurgent's biggest challenge. In order to get at the enemy, "your first object should be the capture of whatever they prize most, and destruction or deprivation of which will probably bring the war most rapidly to a conclusion."[168] Above all, Caldwell cautioned prolonged wars must be avoided as continued public frustration often favors the insurgent. Decisive action, not a "desultory" form of warfare caused by indecisive leadership, half measures, or lack of clear objectives; was the goal.[169] Considering the length of the current struggle between Turkey and the PKK the nearly 20 years of war is an indicator of "desultory" warfare and evidence of the misapplication of counter-insurgency principles. Elements of the Turkish construct have pulled Turkish policy away from the tenets of counter-insurgency and therefore negated the effectiveness of Galula's model as it applied to the Turkish-PKK insurgency.

Galula's model for the operational execution of a counter-insurgency would work if the military and civilian elements were applied in a cohesive fashion. Galula emphasized that counter-insurgency efforts required a single, preferably civilian head and that military action was always secondary to political efforts.[170] Turkish scholars Umit Ozdaz and Ersel Aydinli echoed this sentiment when they wrote, "determination, dedication, and political acumen of both the politicians

---

[168] Caldwell, *Small Wars: Their Principles and Practice*, 40.
[169] Ibid., 99.
[170] Galula, *Counter-Insurgency Warfare: Theory and Practice*, 87.

and military leaders were essential to victory."[171] The military fought a Galula-like campaign, but the non-military means were not integrated. The Turkish Construct, and the Turkish military's role in it, were the inhibitors to this civil-military union.

In relation to Galula's model, the Turkish military campaign does not progress well beyond the first stage. Military resources committed to the campaign were extensive and more than enough to defeat PKK forces in the field. Limited forces were also retained in the southeast to keep insurgents from returning. The Turkish military reinforced these main army units with the Village Guard system that retained nominally loyal organizations in remote villages to protect the citizenry. Beyond these introductory measures, Turkish efforts fall far short of Galula's proscriptions. Its inability to accept the PKK as representing legitimate ethnic discontent hindered the basis on which the Turkish government engaged the population. The political structures implemented after military activity in the region were only extensions of the hated central authorities and advocated one of two courses of action, assimilate or be punished. Winning over converts was nearly impossible.

Lessons – Potential Strategies

The persistent tensions between elements of the Turkish Construct make it difficult to present alternative strategies as any option must satisfy four demanding ideologies. The Turkish government cannot easily withdraw from its hardline stance without sacrificing some principle of Kemalism yet cannot progress along Western lines without shedding undemocratic and intolerant practices that it finds essential to the maintenance of order. Kurdish expert Michael Gunter highlighted another problem when he wrote, "there will generally not be the requisite determination to enact appropriate measures until ethnic conflict has already advanced to a dangerous level; but by that time the measures that are adopted are more likely to be deflected or ineffective."[172] Accepting this argument completely would promote a fatalistic perspective as any future engagement would fail due to

---

[171] Umit Ozdag and Ersel Aydinli, "Winning Low Intensity Conflict: Drawing Lessons from the Turkish Case," 103.

[172] Gunter, *The Kurds and the Future of Turkey*, 75.

irreconcilable differences. In order to resolve the Kurdish question, compromise is essential; however, it must be palatable to all poles of the Turkish Construct.

There are four policies the Turkish government can implement that will greatly assist in addressing the underlying sources of conflict. These are: (1) seek comprehensive and targeted international assistance to revitalize the southeast, (2) develop truly democratic institutions, (3) implement a plan that is integrated across all government agencies, and (4) use local Kurdish institutions to implement the program. Of course, any plan must have the full support of the military and will require a substantial delegation of power by the military elite.

International assistance must be injected into the region without agitating the "Sevres Syndrome".[173] Aid received must not resemble the "Capitulations" or seen as a greater infringement on Turkish sovereignty. The Turkish government must convince the EU any aid package received would be aimed at the Kurdish regions. It may have to suspend EU accession talks until economic conditions in the southeast improve. Considering the current length of the process, a longer wait may not be a large sacrifice. It will also signal to the EU that there exists a strong political will to finally resolve one of the EU's largest reservations to Turkey's membership.

Democratic reforms will be much more difficult to accommodate in the Turkish Construct. Turkish leaders are continually faced with the conundrum of granting greater voice to the populous while needing to maintain control.[174] The primary fear is such freedom will encourage a push away from secularization. Turkish expert Richard Tapper wrote "Islamic movements in modern Turkey are expressions of a search for identity among people who feel their rulers have compromised it by aligning themselves too closely to the West whose values, while seductive, are at the same time both alien and unattainable."[175] Permitting some forms of Kurdish culture to develop and transition into the political process will offer a substitute identity to pure Islamic affiliation Turkish leaders fear so

---

[173] Jung and Piccoli, *Turkey at the Crossroads*, 42.
[174] Radu, ed. *Dangerous Neighborhood*, 210.
[175] Tapper, ed. *Islam in Modern Turkey*, 21.

much. It is a compromise between the needs of Turkish nationalism and secularization. If the words of Iraqi President and renowned Kurdish leader Jalal Talibani are any indication, Turkish Kurd sympathies may be in line with the move to democracy. In an interview with a Turkish newspaper, Talibani declared, "PKK fighting against the current Turkish government amounts to treason against the Kurdish people. This is a terrorist movement…It is against democracy. It is opposed to the democratization process in Turkey. This affair only serves the enemies of the Kurdish people. If they have any sense they will halt this fighting…they should move into the civilian arena and engage in political activity…we are not in the age of Ho Chi Minh and Che Guevara…who does not understand this will pass from the scene."[176] This move to democracy can be aided by a greater, multilateral approach among Turkish government agencies.

An integrated approach, that comprises all elements of national power, is essential. Only when civilian leaders assert some level of control over the reconstruction process can Galula's model actually work. There must be a complementary relationship between security and reconstruction. If military suppression remains the only order of the day, the underlying conditions of discontent will persist. The many plans for such action that have been proposed over the past 20 years must be acted upon.

Finally, an appreciation for Kurdish culture and societal structures can aid Turkey in this process. The Kurds remain a tribally based culture. Where the Ottomans and Kemalists sought to exploit fissures, a new strategy of using these connections to unite tribes may prove more beneficial. If the TOBB report was correct, common interests such as economic opportunities and a level of cultural expression may entice cooperation among Kurds and with Ankara.[177] Based on the new experiences of the Iraqi Kurds, the prestige of such Kurd leaders as Jalal Talibani and Masud Barzani can help craft mutual understanding and cooperation.

---

[176] Yalcin Dogan, "Interview with Iraqi President Talibani on PKK, Ties with Turkey, US," *Istanbul Hurriyet*, 4 September 2005, 1.

[177] Gunter, *The Kurds and the Future of Turkey*, 127.

American policymakers and operational planners should take note of the Turkish campaign for three principal reasons. The first is a cautionary tale of not prizing dogma over pragmatism in formulating policy. The ideological demands of the Turkish Construct allows for only a narrow band of acceptable solutions. A state must execute policies consistent with its cultural norms and societal expectations, but policymakers must also be aware of the realities of the situation. Secondly, policymakers must be aware that understanding the cultural dimensions of the problem are just as important as analyzing the power structures of a state or other political actors. Understanding the power of culture may have allowed Ataturk to co-opt the Kurds by emphasizing Islamic roots and need for economic revitalization through Westernization instead of his rigid enforcement of nationalism. Tailoring the message to cultural sensitivities may dampen the shocks created by changes in the political structure of a state or other political grouping. Policies not informed by cultural realities will meet immediate resistance. Finally, American policymakers and planners must value multi-faceted solutions to complex problems. The Turkish state relied too heavily on a military only approach and failed to address the problem comprehensively from all angles. A broadly based, mutually supporting, and integrated plan encompassing all elements of national power may have not only defeated the PKK, but also resolved the underlying ethnic tensions.

Despite the intensive efforts of the Turkish Republic since 1924, Kurdish nationalism remains a direct threat to the nation's stability. Old tensions between nationalism, Islam, and Westernization, as well as Ottoman traditions, have prevented the creation of an enduring solution. In order to resolve the crisis a compromise is necessary. Appealing to greater international aid focused specifically on the Kurdish problem, encouraging true democracy, developing an integrated approach, and using Kurdish cultural structures to unite and not divide are essential. Only then can a mutual compromise be made to resolve the conflict.

Appendix

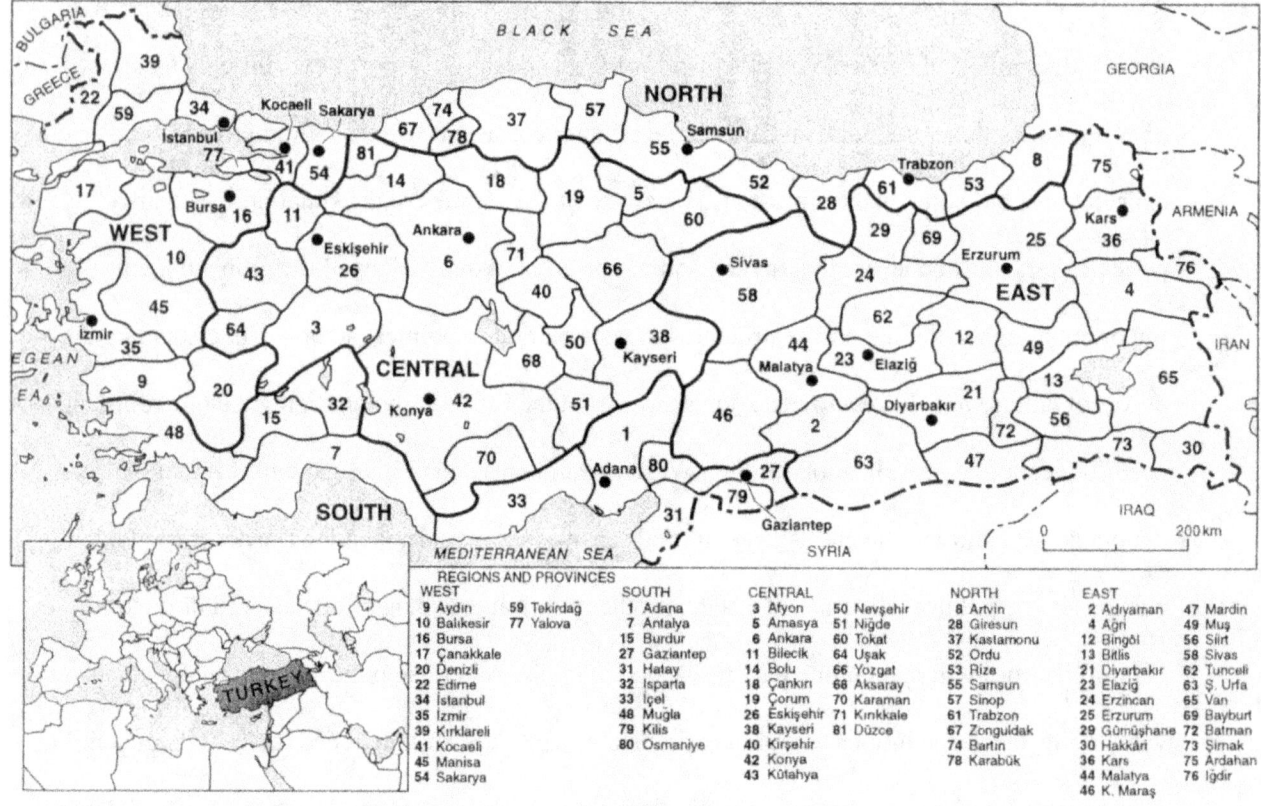

Map of Turkey with Provinces. Source: Brian Beeley, *Turkish Transformation New Century New Challenges*, Cambridge: Eothen, 2002.

Bibliography

Aral, Berdal. "The Idea of Human Rights as Perceived in the Ottoman Empire." *Human Rights Quarterly* 26, no. 2 (May 2004): 454-482.

"A Roadmap from KADEK." *Neu-Isenburg Ozgur Politika*. 12 August 2003.

Aydin, Zulkuf. "Uncompromising Nationalism: The Kurdish Question in Turkey." *The Politics of Permanent Crisis*. Edited by Nesecan Balkan and Sungur Savran. New York: Nova Science, 2002.

Aydinli, Ersel. "Between Security and Liberalization: Decoding Turkey's Struggle with the PKK." *Security Dialogue* 33, no. 2 (June 2002): 209-225.

Balci, Kemal. "RP Plan for Southeast Reported." *Ankara Turkish Daily News*. 23 August 1996.

Bila, Fikret. "Government Gears Up for Action in the Southeast." *Istanbul Milliyet*, 14 September 2000.

_____. "Investment in People." *Istanbul Millayet*. 14 October 2000.

Blank, Steven J., Stephen C. Pelletier, and William T. Johnsen. *Turkey's Strategic Position at the Crossroads of World Affairs*. Carlisle: Strategic Studies Institute, 1993.

van Bruissen, Martin. *Agah, Shaikh and State*. London and New Jersey: Zed Books, 1992.

Caldwell, C. E. *Small Wars: Their Principles and Practice*. Lincoln: University of Nebraska Press, 1996.

Deger, Evren. "Three Messages From the Military of Terror." *Ankara The New Anatolian*. 7 January 2006.

Dodd, C. H. *Democracy and Development in Turkey*. Northgate: Eothen Press, 1979.

Dogan, Yalcin. "Interview with Iraqi President Talibani on PKK, Ties with Turkey, US." *Istanbul Hurriyet*. 4 September 2005.

Donat, Yavuy. "TSK and GAP." *Istanbul Sabah*. 19 February 2002.

Erden, Nuri Sefa. "Turkey's NSC to Discuss Changes in the Southeast." *Istanbul Yeni Yuzyil*. 19 February.

Galula, David. *Counter-Insurgency Warfare: Theory and Practice*. St. Petersburg: Hailer, 2005.

Global Internally Displaced Person Database. "State of Emergency in Southeastern Turkey: Severe Restriction of Human Rights." available from *http://www.db.idpproject.org*.

Griffith, Samuel B. ed. and trans. *On Guerrilla Warfare*. By Mao Tse-tung Urbana and Chicago: University of Illinois Press, 2000.

Gunduz, Aslan. "Turkey and Europe: The Human Rights Conundrum." In *Dangerous Neighborhood.*, Edited by Michael S. Radu. New Brunswick: Transaction, 2003.

Gunter, Michael M. *The Kurds and the Future of Turkey*. New York: St. Martin's, 1997.

_____. *The Kurds in Turkey: A Political Dilemma*. Boulder: Westview Press, 1990.

Hale, William. *Turkish Politics and the Military*. New York: Routledge, 1994.

Heper, Metin, and Aylin Guney. "The Military and the Consolidation of Democracy: The Recent Turkish Experience." *Armed Forces and Society* 26, no. 4 (Summer 2000): 635-657.

Houston, Christopher. *Islam, Kurds and the Turkish Nation State.* Oxford: Berg, 2001.

Inbar, Afrain. "Turkey's New Strategic Partner Israel," In *Dangerous Neighborhood*. Edited by Michael Radu. New Brunswick: Transaction, 2003.

Jacoby, Tim. "For the People, Of the People, and by the Military: The Regime Structure of Modern Turkey." *Political Studies* 51 (2003): 669-685.

Jung, Dietrich, and Wolfgang Piccoli. *Turkey at the Crossroads*, London and New York: Zed Books, 2001.

Larrabee, Stephen. "US and European Policy Towards Turkey and the Caspian Basin." In *Allies Divided*. Edited by Robert Blackwell and Michael Sturmer. Cambridge: MIT Press, 1997.

Lewis, Bernard. *The Emergence of Modern Turkey*, 2nd Ed. Oxford: Oxford University Press, 1969.

McCarthey, Justin. *The Ottoman Turks.* New York: Longman, 1997.

McDowell, David. *A Modern History of the Kurds*, 3rd Ed. New York: St. Martin's, 2005.

Nachmani, Amikam. *Turkey: Facing a New Millennium.* Manchester and New York: Manchester University Press, 2003.

Olson, Robert. *The Emergence of Kurdish Nationalism and the Sheik Said Rebellion, 1880-1925.* Austin: University of Texas Press, 1989.

_____., ed. *The Kurdish National Movement in the 1990s*. Lexington: University Press of Kentucky, 1996.

Ozdag, Umit, and Ersel Aydinli. "Winning Low Intensity Conflict: Drawing Lessons from the Turkish Case." *Review of International Affairs* 2, no. 3 (Spring 2003): 101-121.

Oztekin, Yuksel. "Terrorism in Turkey." Masters Thesis, US Army War College, 2000.

"Prime Minister Edrogan in Diyarbakir." *Ankara Anatolian* 12 August 2005

Radu, Michael., ed. *Dangerous Neighborhood.* New Brunswick: Transaction, 2003.

_____. "The Rise and Fall of the PKK." *Orbis.* 45, no. 2 (Winter 2001): 47-55.

Republic of Turkey. 1990. *Decree 430*. 16 December 1990; available from http://www.law.qub.ac.uk/humanrts/emergency/turkey/tur7.htm.

Republic of Turkey. 1993. *State of Emergency Law Act 2935*. 25 October 1993; available from http://www.law.qub.ac.uk/humanrts/emergency/turkey/tur4.htm.

Richard Tapper, ed. *Islam in Modern Turkey.* London and New York: I. B. Taurus, 1991.

Robins, Philip. "The Overlord State: Turkish Policy and the Kurdish Issue." *International Affairs* 69, no. 4 (October 1993): 657-676.

Speech of Olli Rehn to EU-Turkey Joint Parliamentary Committee, 23 November 2005. *Brussels Rapid Database*, Brussels.

Terrorism Knowledge Database. "HPG." available from http://www.tKb.org.

"The PKK and Ethnic Terrorism in Turkey." *Ankara Papers* 9, no. 1 (January 2004): 1-20.

Toprak, Binnaz. "Islam and Democracy in Turkey." *Turkish Studies* 6, no. 2, (June 2005): 167-186.

Tse-tung, Mao. *On Guerrilla War*. Edited and translated by Samuel B. Griffith. Urbana and Chicago: University of Illinois Press, 2000.

Turabian, Kate L. *A Manual for Writers of Term Papers, Theses, and Dissertations*. 6th ed. Chicago: University of Chicago Press, 1996.

Turan, Ilter. "Religion and Political Culture in Turkey," In *Islam in Modern Turkey*. Edited by Richard Tapper. London and New York: I. B. Taurus and Company, 1991.

White, Paul. *Primitive Rebels or Revolutionary Modernizers?* New York: Zed Books, 2000.

Yesilada, Birol A. "Turkish-US Relations." In *Dangerous Neighborhood*. Edited by Michael S. Radu. New Brunswick: Transaction, 2003.

Yilmaz, Sinan. "Chamber of Commerce Report on Kurds Detailed." *Ankara Turkish Daily News*, 4 August 1995, A2.